# INTIMATE WARFARE

# INTIMATE WARFARE

## *The True Story of the Arturo Gatti and Micky Ward Boxing Trilogy*

**Dennis Taylor**
**John J. Raspanti**

ROWMAN & LITTLEFIELD
Lanham • Boulder • New York • London

Published by Rowman & Littlefield
A wholly owned subsidiary of The Rowman & Littlefield Publishing Group, Inc.
4501 Forbes Boulevard, Suite 200, Lanham, Maryland 20706
www.rowman.com

Unit A, Whitacre Mews, 26-34 Stannary Street, London SE11 4AB

British Library Cataloguing in Publication Information Available

**Library of Congress Cataloging-in-Publication Data**

Names: Taylor, Dennis, 1953– author. | Raspanti, John J., 1958– author.
Title: Intimate warfare : the true story of the Arturo Gatti and Micky Ward boxing trilogy / Dennis Taylor and John J. Raspanti.
Description: Lanham, Maryland : Rowman & Littlefield, 2017. | Includes bibliographical references and index. | Description based on print version record and CIP data provided by publisher; resource not viewed.
Identifiers: LCCN 2016037648 (print) | LCCN 2016021159 (ebook) | ISBN 9781442273061 (electronic) | ISBN 9781442273054 (hardback : alk. paper)
Subjects: LCSH: Gatti, Arturo, 1972-2009. | Ward, Micky. | Boxing—History—21st century. | Boxers (Sports)—Biography.
Classification: LCC GV1132.G36 (print) | LCC GV1132.G36 T39 2017 (ebook) | DDC 796.830922 [B] —dc23
LC record available at https://lccn.loc.gov/2016037648

♾ ™ The paper used in this publication meets the minimum requirements of American National Standard for Information Sciences Permanence of Paper for Printed Library Materials, ANSI/NISO Z39.48-1992.

Printed in the United States of America

For our fathers, who were boxing fans

# CONTENTS

# FOREWORD

## Ray "Boom Boom" Mancini

**W**hen I think of the Gatti–Ward trilogy, many adjectives come to mind: violent, brutal, fierce, passionate, powerful, raging, savage, vicious. Yet, if you had met either or both men, you would have known that most of the words used to describe their fights were the complete opposite of their personalities and personas. Both men exemplified the words *courageous*, *honorable*, and *virtuous* inside the ring, as well as, *gentlemanly*, *noble*, and *gracious* outside of it. They were everything that is good about the "fight game." They were benevolent men.

As hard as they went after one another in their fights, trying to beat the other into oblivion, it was with the same intensity and strength that they forged a friendship and bond that will never be severed. The mutual respect and admiration they had for one another and, later, dare I say, the love that they developed for one another, were something that only men of their substance and character could feel and understand. Only men who have gone through the turbulent and tumultuous rounds that they did could understand such a bond.

*Warriors*, *gladiators*, and *combatants* are words often used to describe Gatti and Ward, and their pugilistic styles. Inevitably, the word *champion* follows, to emphasize who and what they are, to their fans, to the game, and to the world at large.

I don't know if we will ever see another series of fights between two men with the same intensity, ferocity, and drama that these two staged inside the ring—or the same grace, dignity, and decency that they showed one another outside of it.

As a fan of both men, of who they were, what they accomplished, and the great memories they left behind, I want to congratulate them, for their achievements, for their success, and for the immortality they attained through the series of fights that you are about to read about.

*Ray "Boom Boom" Mancini is a former World Boxing Association light-weight champion. He was inducted into the International Boxing Hall of Fame in 2015.*

# ACKNOWLEDGMENTS

*This book is dedicated to our fathers, who were boxing fans.*

## ROBERT N. TAYLOR (1918–2009)

I was small enough to fit on my dad's lap when I fell in love with boxing, and that might have been where I sat on March 24, 1962—eight days after my ninth birthday—when my favorite fighter, Emile Griffith, fought Benny "Kid" Paret for the third time at New York's Madison Square Garden. That welterweight championship fight was televised live by ABC, and Dad and I watched it on our scratchy, old Magnavox TV, toward which I would occasionally be nudged to adjust the rabbit ears.

I recall feeling mortified when Paret nearly KO'd Griffith halfway through the fight—my guy was saved by the bell in the sixth—then celebrating wildly when Griffith unleashed an avalanche of punches (29 in a row, they figured out later, 18 in a six-second span) to finish Paret in the 12th.

The tragedy, of course, is that Paret died days later from the injuries he sustained that night. I remember seeing his photo in the *Denver Post*, thinking Paret looked like a little boy. I felt bad and suddenly understood that boxing was a very serious sport.

Why I remained enamored remained a mystery for some time, and then I figured it out. So did my dad, who was the gentlest man I ever knew. He also was one of the toughest people I've known—a Depression-era guy who grew up on the north side of Pittsburgh, in a neighborhood where, he liked to claim, "We played dodgeball with half a brick . . . and nobody cheated."

Dad was a little guy—a shade under 5-foot-7, 150 pounds—whose own father owned an illegal Pittsburgh speakeasy until hard times hit. So, he moved his family to a cheaper, meaner side of town, where, on their first day in the new neighborhood, my dad and his older brother, Richard, stepped outside to play catch with a football.

As Dad told the tale, a neighborhood tough guy named Chuck Short leapt from bushes, intercepted the ball, and took off down Tweed Street like Red Grange. The Taylor boys chased him down, and since Richard was older and much larger, Dad had to fight to get the ball back. (There was honor among fistfighters in those days.) Long story short, the hero of this story whupped Chuck Short's ass, got the football, and walked Tweed Street with some semblance of street cred from that day onward.

By the way, I believe every word of his tale. My father was an intensely honest and honorable man—never prone to fabrication or exaggeration, unless his tongue was in his cheek.

His brother Richard, an uncle I never met, dabbled as an amateur fighter in Pittsburgh and was an occasional sparring partner for the Zivic brothers—there were five, including Fritzie, who owned the world welterweight championship in 1940 and 1941. By then, Uncle Richard was a paratrooper, fighting the Japanese in the South Pacific. He came home from the war with at least one magnificent confession: Richard and a buddy had become separated from their unit during one wild battle and had ducked into a cave to hide. That's where they found a treasure trove of Japanese beer. Uncle Richard came home with a Purple Heart and a drinking problem, but the Congressional Medal of Honor somehow eluded him.

Dad served in the U.S. Navy during the war but never left the States, mostly making pancakes for his fellow sailors—apparently delicious ones: He was discharged with honor and returned to Pittsburgh to become a trolley car operator (a broken-down Honus Wagner, legendary Pirates shortstop, was a frequent, very drunk, late-night passenger) before bringing his family West.

That's when I came along, the third of four kids to breathe the comforting scent of his undershirt as I sat with him during fights, or ballgames, or *Car 54, Where Are You?*. As I grew, Dad and I continued to share boxing experiences. He took me to Denver to watch an amateur team called the Denver Rocks, whose lineup included a heavyweight named Ron Lyle.

In 1996, after I had become a sportswriter, I took Dad to see Buddy McGirt—well past his prime—sleepwalk through the second-to-last fight of his career. And during his last year, my father was a dedicated reader of the articles I wrote for four daily newspapers and a big fan of *The Ringside Boxing Show*, which I have hosted since 2008.

Dad was battling four different kinds of cancer when he died in 2009, so I was happy—not sad—when he died suddenly of a heart attack while relaxing in a hot tub. He was already grinning his way through physical discomforts that I'll mercifully decline to describe here, and I knew what was coming: Dad was a fighter who, like most fighters, would have battled too long. This was better.

If there's a heaven, hopefully they've got a bookstore or a library, because I'm pretty sure he would have enjoyed *Intimate Warfare: The True Story of the Arturo Gatti and Micky Ward Boxing Trilogy*.

One final note: My father's favorite boxer during the latter years of his life, Ray "Boom Boom" Mancini, wrote the foreword for this book.

RIP, dear ol' Dad. I love you.

—Dennis Taylor

## JOHN J. RASPANTI SR. (1927–2013)

My dad loved boxing. His favorite fighter was the legendary "Brown Bomber," Joe Louis. He had heard about Louis when he was seven years old, on the streets of Chicago, Illinois, near the small house he shared with his parents and six siblings.

Dad loved to tell me about the most important night of his life. The date was June 22, 1937. His hero, Joe Louis, was set to fight the heavyweight champion of the world, the "Cinderella Man," James J. Braddock. The venue was Comiskey Park, home of the Chicago White Sox baseball team, located just five blocks from where my dad lived. This was his chance to see Louis live and in person. No more just reading about him in the papers. He had one big problem. It would cost money to see the fight. On a good day, my Dad might have had a nickel in his pocket.

No matter. He was going. He walked to Comiskey, trying to figure out how he would get into the park. Maybe he could slide past the ticket-takers by hiding behind an adult. No, they'd see him. He was skinny but pretty tall for his age. The entire area around the park was packed with cars. Lights blazed around him. Excitement was in the air.

As he neared the park, he could see two ominous figures standing near the entrance. Men in suits milled about. He looked to his left, trying to find the other entrance, where he had sold papers a few months before. It was closed. He kept walking, willing himself to be invisible. The ticket guys were talking to each other. He heard a roar from inside the park.

Had the Louis–Braddock fight started? He walked faster. Maybe they wouldn't see him.

"Hey," said a voice. "Where do you think you're going?"

Dad stopped. They had caught him. He could see the bright lights of the park straight ahead. He was so close. He looked to where the voice had come from and saw a man, who was older, fat, and not smiling, with a younger ticket-taker beside him. He wasn't smiling either.

"I just want to see the Louis fight," Dad said.

He heard another roar from the park as he waited impatiently, looking up at the older man. Suddenly, my father saw the man's eyes soften.

"You go ahead son," he said.

Dad smiled and ran as fast as he could into the park. He stood in the aisle, overhearing someone say that round 8 was about to begin. He had never seen so many people in one place. When the bell rang, he studied Louis as he stalked Braddock. He felt nervous, remembering how Louis had been knocked out by Max Schmeling the year before.

That was then.

In the blink of an eye, a heavy right hand sent Braddock to the canvas. He never moved a muscle as the referee counted over him. Old Comiskey Park shook as my dad and rest of the fans roared.

A few years later, Dad competed in the Chicago Golden Gloves. He won most of his bouts—employing a slick boxing style and stinging right hand. He was good enough that a local manager wanted him to turn professional. Dad rejected the offer and joined the U.S. Army instead.

I discovered boxing in the 1960s. At last, Dad could share his stories with someone. He would amaze me with his tales of seeing boxing greats Sugar Ray Robinson, Ike Williams, Johnny Bratton, and Kid Gavilan at the same pool hall in Chicago. He told me about seeing one of his favorites, Rocky Graziano, defeat Tony Zale at Chicago Stadium, as his eyes misted and a smile lit up his face.

When I was a teenager he took me to the hallowed Olympic Auditorium in Los Angeles. I was mesmerized by the lobby—filled with pictures of some of boxing's greatest. Dad smiled and nodded, acknowledging my passion for the "sweet science." That passion never dimmed for either of us. The last time we spoke, we spent most of our time discussing boxing.

I only wish he were here now to read *Intimate Warfare: The True Story of the Arturo Gatti and Micky Ward Boxing Trilogy*. I have to believe that with the same spirit he showed as a nine-year-old determined to see his idol, Joe Louis, my dad will find a way.

Love and miss you, Dad.

—John J. Raspanti

# PROLOGUE

The end. Such a sad place for a story to begin.

Arturo Gatti was just 37 years old the night he died, July 11, 2009, in the fancy beachfront room he was renting in Ipojuca, Pernambuco, Brazil, where he and his wife, Amanda Rodrigues, were attempting to reignite a spark in their struggling marriage.

Brazilian police initially arrested Amanda and charged her with murder, but then, in a fog of confusion and suspicion that still exists today, they released her and concluded that one of the greatest blood-and-guts boxers of all time had committed suicide by hanging.

Most of Gatti's family and friends don't believe that. Although he was prone to mood swings and occasionally drank too much—as he had on the night of his death—those closest to Gatti insist that taking his own life was an option he never would have considered. Among the most adamant is a person who had come to know Gatti on a more intimate level than anyone else in his life.

Micky Ward, Gatti's opponent in three of the most spectacular and violent fights ever seen, cast doubt on the theory that his close friend had committed suicide.

"I never believed that he did that, that he took his own life—never," Ward said in an emotionally charged speech at a ceremony enshrining Gatti into the International Boxing Hall of Fame. "He had a son [Arturo Jr.] that he loved to death. He had a daughter, Sofia, that he loved to death. Two kids. He wouldn't do it. No way. I don't see it."

Sofia, from a previous relationship, was three when her father died. Arturo Jr., born to Amanda and Arturo just 10 months before his father's death, was with his parents in Brazil.

But Ward had another reason to reject the suicide theory. He knew Gatti as someone who, much like himself, was a fighter, a gladiator who had never given up on anything in his life —a man who, in Ward's mind, never would.

Micky Ward, a sandpaper-rough Irishman from the faded and depressed industrial city of Lowell, Massachusetts, met handsome, charismatic, former world champion Arturo Gatti in the ring for the first time on May 18, 2002, at the Mohegan Sun Casino in Uncasville, Connecticut, where they engaged in a brawl so close and so brutal that it is permanently ensconced near the top of every credible "Fights of the Century" list.

The rematch, held six months later at Boardwalk Hall in Atlantic City, proved worthy of the hype generated by its predecessor. The "rubber match," which took place in June 2003, at the same venue, tied a majestic bow on a gift to boxing fans that may very well rate as the most sensational trilogy of pugilism ever contested.

Three fights, 30 rounds, no title belts at stake. They beat one another bloody, closed one another's eyes, broke one another's bones. Ward and Gatti didn't need to fight for trinkets—there was so much more at stake. They did it, very simply, because they owed it to themselves, to one another, and to their fans.

# Part I

# Collision Course

# I

# "I ALWAYS WONDERED WHAT IT WOULD BE LIKE TO FIGHT MY TWIN"

**A**t the end of their third and final fight, Micky Ward and Arturo Gatti were transported separately to the same Atlantic City hospital to be checked out by emergency-room doctors. Ward, who lost the fight, had a tennis ball–sized lump under his left eye, an inch-long slash above his left eyebrow, and a bloody dent across the bridge of his nose. He also had been suffering from blurred double- and triple-vision since the third round (permanent damage that still affects him today).

"There's something wrong with my eyes!" he had told his brother Dicky between rounds.

"What?"

"There's something wrong with my eyes!" Ward repeated. "I can't see! I'm seeing three of him out there!"

"Hit the one in the middle!" his unsympathetic brother/trainer advised before sending Micky out for round 4.[1]

Doctors at the ER found Gatti's right hand in pieces. He had broken that hand multiple times in his career, including both previous fights with Ward. Doctors pieced it back together after their first fight, 13 months earlier, bolting the bones to a titanium plate. That plate came loose during their second fight and had to be surgically repaired again. And now, the hand had been shattered yet again, this time by a punch Gatti had driven into Ward's hip just 30 seconds into the fourth round.

"They may end up having to stop the fight," observed Hall of Fame trainer Emanuel Steward, analyzing the bout at ringside for HBO. "This is what makes boxing different from all other sports. In any other sport, you could call a timeout and substitute another athlete. You can't do it in boxing. The whole team is Gatti."

Gatti tested the injury with a handful of tentative punches, wincing noticeably each time. When the bell ended the round, Gatti slumped onto his stool and buried his face in the shoulder of his trainer, Buddy McGirt.

"I broke my right hand," Gatti confided, a secret barely audible to HBO's prying microphone.

"What do you want me to do?" McGirt asked.

"I'm going to keep going."

McGirt, a former world champion himself, said nothing more. He didn't have to. The great ones have a secret compartment—a lockbox— where they hide pain during a fight. Simply said, it's not a high priority. The great ones will worry about it later, when it's throbbing in the middle of the night, night after night. What matters, instead, is that there's a raging werewolf in the opposite corner who, when the bell rings in a few short seconds, will do everything in his power to wreak more havoc.

During the final seven rounds, Gatti had ignored the agony and psychology of the injury and never stopped using the right to batter his opponent.

"There has been nothing like this series in boxing since [Riddick] Bowe and [Evander] Holyfield a decade ago," HBO commentator Larry Merchant opined during a spectacular seventh round.

"This is better," Steward answered. "This is better."

"The most overused word in sports commentary is 'incredible,'" added Jim Lampley, HBO's blow-by-blow specialist. "This is an incredible fight."

After stitching up Ward and searching his eyes for signs of brain hemorrhages and clues to his vision problems, doctors wheeled him into a triage area, leaving him beneath a stack of ice packs with an IV rehydrating his spent body.

"Hey, Mick . . . you okay, brother?"[2]

Ward peeked out from beneath an ice pack and was surprised to see Arturo Gatti grinning at him through swollen lips from the next gurney. Gatti's left eye was every bit as puffy and discolored as Ward's.

"Yeah, man, I'm fine . . . how 'bout you?"

Gatti nodded and offered a thumbs up.

It's a curiosity about boxing that few outsiders can fully understand. Two fighters spend 10 or 12 rounds with only one thing in mind—obliterating one another. In many cases, they do whatever seems necessary at the time—a shot to the gonads, a punch to the stem of the brain, an "errant" elbow to the eye socket, a missile to the kidney—often on the heels of weeks of prefight posturing, during which each fighter has repeatedly demeaned the other, questioning his manhood and itemizing his perceived weaknesses and flaws to the media and anyone else who might listen. Sometimes it gets so personal and ugly that one fighter will insult the other's family.

Benny "Kid" Paret repeatedly called Emile Griffith "maricon"—Spanish slang for homosexual—then grabbed Griffith's buttocks before their 1962 fight at New York's Madison Square Garden. Griffith unleashed such rage and inflicted so much damage on his opponent during the 12th round of the fight that Paret faded into a coma and died 10 days later.

Sugar Ray Leonard and Roberto Duran nearly came to blows on a Montreal street after Duran insulted Ray's wife, interrupting an otherwise pleasant prefight stroll.

A frustrated Mike Tyson famously bit off Evander Holyfield's ear in the heat of battle during their second meeting in 1997.

Nothing like that had ever happened when Gatti fought Ward. If a punch strayed low or speared a kidney, it was mostly by accident. If a reporter baited either fighter to taunt or diminish the other at a press conference, neither Ward nor Gatti would bite. They respected one another. They admired one another. They even came to love one another, the way one brother loves the other.

"Hell of a fight, huh?" Ward said, as he waited for a doctor to piece his flesh together again.

Gatti smiled. "We gotta start getting paid more for this."

Micky Ward's name appears among the first paragraphs in every version of Arturo Gatti's obituary. Like Abbott and Costello, Barnum and Bailey, Masters and Johnson, either name would be incomplete without the other.

It's a trait that recurs in boxing because of the very nature of the sport, which is one-on-one: Muhammad Ali's legacy would not be the same without Joe Frazier. Joe Louis became a historic figure in part because of Max Schmeling. Sugar Ray Robinson's legend grew from his epic wars with Jake LaMotta.

When they're done trying to vaporize one another, boxers commonly do what Ward and Gatti did when they heard the bell that ended their third spectacular war: They embraced for several seconds, paying a deep, heartfelt homage to an opponent who had challenged them like no one else, pushing them closer to oblivion than they ever imagined was possible.

When the bell sounded to end their third and final war, Gatti and Ward spent several very intimate seconds in a weary, sweat-drenched embrace, whispering sweet nothings, while a worldwide television audience observed. What was said? It doesn't matter. Whatever they shared at that moment was too personal for the rest of us to appreciate.

"I always wondered what it would be like to fight my twin," Gatti said later. "Now I know."[3]

Archrivals develop a bond through mortal combat that only they can feel. They have their nemesis to thank for the greatness they have achieved. They will be linked in history and mythology for the rest of their natural lives and beyond, like Doc Holliday and Johnny Ringo.

Ward and Gatti will be remembered as mortal men who, mostly through courage and sheer will, accomplished things before our very eyes that should not have been humanly possible. They pushed themselves beyond those physical limits that the rest of us have come to accept, past the fatigue, the agony, the fear, the nagging desire to give up, rest, and save at least part of themselves for another day. None of those things was an option for either man. And they did it three times.

The postscript to their epic trilogy is that an enduring friendship developed between the two men, a bond whose deep roots can be traced to those 30 brutal rounds. They became confidants, seeking one another's advice, often in the wee hours of the morning. They were occasionally golfing buddies. People close to both fighters said they quite literally developed their own language when they talked on the phone.

Ward retired as a boxer immediately after their third fight. Gatti fought on, entering the ring seven more times. Poetically, he hired Ward as his trainer for the final fight of his career.

Without Arturo Gatti, Micky Ward's footprint in boxing would have been minor. He was appreciated as a reliable action fighter of limited ability, and entirely too much courage, who could usually be counted on by one of the second-tier boxing networks to provide formidable competition for opponents perceived to have a brighter future. He was what boxing insiders call a "stepping-stone" or a "gatekeeper." And until he crossed paths with Gatti, Ward was an ESPN-level fighter, not quite special enough to make the jump to the HBO stage, where the big-leaguers (which included Gatti) showcased their skills.

Without Ward, a portion of Gatti's legacy would have endured—he was, after all, a three-time world champion whose nicknames (aside from "Thunder") included the "Human Highlight Reel" and the "Blood and Guts Warrior." His thrilling, never-quit style earned him 19 appearances on HBO.

But his trilogy against Ward nudged him into another stratosphere in the sport, into that rarified air reserved only for folk heroes. Their collaboration elevated them to a special list that includes Robinson and LaMotta, Pep and Saddler, Graziano and Zale, Barrera and Morales, and other duos who, had their paths never crossed, would have been significantly less memorable to fans and historians. Together, Gatti and Ward summited boxing's Mount Olympus, a place neither could have found without the other.

# 2

# MICKY

Micky Ward grew up rough in Lowell, Massachusetts, a depressed, blue-collar Boston suburb whose streets were filthy with drug dealers, drunks, thugs, and prostitutes. His neighborhood, known as the "Acre," may have been the roughest in the city. Against all odds, Ward somehow managed to avoid most of the pitfalls that eventually sunk his older half-brother, Dicky Eklund, a bona fide prospect who destroyed his career with alcohol, crack cocaine, and street violence, all of which put him on a first-name basis at the city and county lockups, and eventually two different state prisons.

Ward was perpetually wide-eyed around his brother, who at 15 was already an accomplished amateur star in New England. Dicky had similarly worshiped their two brothers-in-law, Beau Jaynes, who had married their sister Donna, and Larry Carney, husband of their sister Gail, each of whom had significant natural ability and stellar amateur careers. Micky wasn't as talented as his big brother, but he proved to be far more dedicated to boxing than Dicky, or, for that matter, either of his brothers-in-law.

Carney had come first. He was born in Lowell in 1939, turned pro in 1961, and fought for 11 years, mostly at middleweight and light heavyweight. He won the USA New England middleweight title in 1963 and the light heavyweight version of that same belt in 1967. Carney went 28–11, with 19 KOs (after a 14–1 start), as a pro. Carney's best weapon in the ring was a vaunted left hook, and his vulnerabilities included addictions to beer, ice cream, and late-night parties. He didn't count calories when he was training, nor did he burn very many in the gym. Like many in Lowell, Carney fell prey to alcoholism and, in 1992, died from head injuries sustained in a tumble down a flight of stairs.

"He loved to fight, whether it was in the ring or on the street," according to local historian Christine Lewis. "You won't find this on Carney's official record, but his most talked-about fight in Lowell occurred when he punched a certain local heavyweight across the street and almost into the canal. A certain status is bestowed upon men who can legitimately claim they were there."[1]

Beau Jaynes, whose given name was Bobby, came along later. He was born in Lowell in 1945, made his pro debut in 1965, and fought for money 97 times (after 160 amateur fights), ultimately losing almost as many as he won (45 defeats). But his record belies his talent. Jaynes, who grew up in the "Acre," became the only man in history to hold New England championships in five weight divisions, all at the same time. He was simultaneously the region's belt-holder at featherweight, junior lightweight, lightweight, junior welterweight, and welterweight, gaining and losing weight for every title fight. Jaynes's pro career included fights with Sean O'Grady, Tony Petronelli, Leo Randolph, Mando Ramos, and Antonio Cervantes. Jaynes said his most memorable fights were back-to-back brawls with an unbeaten opponent in 1968, when he was New England's lightweight champion.

"I fought and lost a 12-round bout to Ken Campbell. He had 40 wins and zero losses after the fight," Jaynes told a local reporter in Lowell. "We agreed to fight again six weeks later. We fought, and I got my New England title back by knocking him out in seven rounds. I used a left hook to knock him down. It felt great. He never fought again after that."[2]

Jaynes's star began to fade in 1974, when he lost a 10-round unanimous decision to Marvin Hagler's future cotrainer, Tony Petronelli (who, two years later, would lose to Wilfred Benitez in a WBA light welterweight title bout). That loss began a downward spiral during which Jaynes was beaten 23 times in 30 fights, including the last eight bouts of his career.

Jaynes worked 34 years for the Department of Public Works in Lowell, but his local star power never quite faded away. "Everywhere I go people wave to me. When I'm on a run, people honk at me. It is nice to be known. It is a lot of fun," he once said.[3]

Ward, just a second grader when he began boxing, never watched either Carney or Jaynes in their heydays, but Dicky idolized both men and aspired to follow in their footsteps. They took him under their wings and helped him develop as an amateur fighter.

Dicky lived as a local superstar for a few years, compiling an amateur record of 194–6. As a pro, he was good enough to survive a 10-round fight with future Hall of Famer Sugar Ray Leonard in 1978. Eklund, Jaynes, and Carney each took turns on their knees, absorbing haymaker punches from little Micky, who began taking instruction from Art Ramalho at the West End Gym when he was seven years old.

Arthur Ramalho's West End Gym, on Middlesex Street, sat in another hardscrabble section of Lowell known as the "Grove." The gym was hidden in one of the countless abandoned textile mills that, in another era, had made the city an industrial hub. (Lowell is widely hailed as the birthplace of the American Industrial Revolution.)

Ramalho, whose son David also was an accomplished Lowell boxer, remembered watching a pint-sized Micky trailing along as his big brother showed up at the gym for a workout one day. Micky was dragging Dicky's athletic bag—a bag nearly as big as he was, Ramalho recollected. That was the beginning.

The crusty "Mr. Ramalho" ran the busy gym with the help of various other boxing rats, including Mickey Carney (Larry's brother), who became Micky's first "trainer," teaching him how to properly wrap his hands and shadowbox. Micky sparred regularly, even at seven, against almost anyone close to his weight or age and had his first live fight before his eighth birthday against Joey Roach, younger brother of now-legendary trainer Freddie Roach (an amateur star by then).

Micky remembers absorbing a hard punch square in the face within the first 10 seconds of his fight with Roach and immediately hitting him back. The fight lasted a round and a half before a cloudburst drowned both kids and the spectators, and made the ring too slippery to continue. Both kids got their arms raised and went home with a trophy.

Joey Roach went on to have a solid amateur career and then went 8–3–3 as a pro bantamweight, scoring three knockouts against nondescript opposition.

From that day onward—and probably before—Micky was in love with almost everything about the sport, right down to the rank smell of the gym. Most compelling, however, was the privilege of tagging along almost every day with his big brother—eight years older—a local celebrity who was both feared and revered.

Micky dropped out of high school as a junior, exceeding Dicky's education by three years. By that time, he was already locally famous as a Golden Gloves champion, but the street life that had lured so many young people into ruin in Lowell was also threatening to take Micky Ward. He often drank with friends until just before sunrise and didn't shy away from the occasional booze-fueled street brawl, which would send him home bloody and bruised, often with hand injuries that would bother him throughout his pro career.

Tony Underwood, Micky's cousin, remembers Lowell's police force as less than helpful when a middle-of-the-night rumble would erupt on the city streets. The combatants—Micky included—often took a worse beating from the cops than they did from one another, he recounted.

Micky spent his days working for his uncle, paving Lowell's streets and parking lots or hammering nails for his father's roofing company. He trained at night, usually with big brother Dicky at his side as his trainer. But Dicky's drug and alcohol addictions often rendered Micky's training camps dysfunctional and inefficient. Many nights he was nowhere to be found, unless Micky went prowling through the local crack houses (which he sometimes did).

That dysfunction extended to his management team, which was composed entirely of his mom, Alice Eklund-Ward, a strong-willed woman who called the shots, deciding which fights her son took and what he got paid. She had done the same for Jaynes, Carney, and Dicky—admittedly with minimal effectiveness, not only because her decision-making was erratic, but also because she was a female pioneer trying to navigate the unsympathetic and grotesquely bigoted all-male world of professional boxing. Far too often, Ward found himself overmatched and undercompensated when the bell rang.

To his credit and detriment, Ward seldom, if ever, criticized her decisions. It was in his DNA to fight Godzilla, if that's who showed up at the weigh-in, and the modest paycheck he received seemed perfectly normal to someone who had grown accustomed to the no-frills, no-sympathy, blue-collar life of Lowell. People there woke up each morning with the expectation that life was meant to be hard and that "good luck" usually happened to someone else.

Alice Eklund-Ward was the mother of seven girls and two boys. Her first seven children, including Dicky—born third—were fathered by Dick Eklund. The two youngest, including Micky, were sired by her second husband, George Ward. Every kid in the clan had a nickname: Donna, the oldest, was called "Stemp"; second-born Gail was known as "Red Dog"; Dicky was "Bird"; Phyllis was "Beaver"; Cindy was "Tar"; Kathy was "Pork"; and Alice, the last of the Eklunds, was "Bagels." George Ward's first child, Micky, was nicknamed "Bear Head," and Sherrie, the baby of the family, became "Dirty Sally."

In his autobiography *A Warrior's Heart* (coauthored by *New York Times* journalist Joe Layden), Ward is unable to offer an origin for any of the monikers, but he believed that most, or all, could be traced to physical characteristics.

Theirs was a loud, emotional, often-volatile family—and extended family. Regular family outings at a nearby lake began with a barbecue, softball, and horseshoes, but inevitably degenerated into at least one beer-fueled fistfight between members of the Ward clan, often women. Micky, Dicky, cousins, and friends pulled their lawn chairs ringside to observe the carnage with equal parts astonishment and amusement. Then, with the blood drying and the bruises on ice, it was back to the beer and barbecue.

The story of Micky Ward cannot be told without describing the turbulent world that swirled around him throughout his life. Any young man growing up in Lowell, Massachusetts, 30 minutes from Boston, could be likened to a small boat trying to sail through a typhoon, battling an endless assault of perilous, unpredictable waves.

The city was named after Francis Cabot Lowell, inventor of weaving machines that spawned a bustling industrial city at the intersection of two formidable rivers—the Merrimack and the Concord. Six miles of canals sprouted in every direction, providing arteries that fed 40 textile mills during the heyday of the city, which was the second largest in New England in the mid-1800s. But by the mid-1920s, textile mills were relocating to the southern United States, where the cotton was grown, and, as the Great Depression took hold, Lowell fell on hard times.

The streets Micky Ward navigated as a seven-year-old, riding his bicycle each day from his home to Arthur Ramalho's West End Gym, were a labyrinth of drunks, drug addicts, prostitutes, hustlers, and other dangerous desperadoes. This survival-of-the-fittest habitat wore people down until they broke from anger, frustration, stress, financial strife, racial tension, and the allure of self-medication, which, for many, seemed like the only way to deal with it all.

Both Ward and his half-brother Dicky applauded the general accuracy of the feature film *The Fighter*, which earned great critical acclaim, as well as box-office success. Actor Christian Bale won an Oscar for his portrayal of the crack-addicted Eklund. Another Hollywood A-lister, native New Englander Mark Wahlberg, starred as Ward.

Lowell was a place where drug and alcohol abuse were part of the culture. By the time Ward was 14, he and his friends would sometimes drink until closing time at any of at least four local taverns where the bartenders would happily serve them a beer. Not surprisingly, parking-lot fights also were a nightly attraction. By all accounts, Ward was a good-natured, friendly kid, but he also was someone who decided at a very young age that he'd never back away from a fight.

"We've seen years and years of street fights with Micky. Very rarely did Micky ever lose a street fight," remembered his cousin, Tony Underwood. "He probably weighed like 130 pounds back then, and he took on some 200-pounders, but Micky would always win."[4]

Ward has fond memories of shadowing his brother everywhere, walking with him to a local train station, sitting alongside him as they rode from Lowell to Poston, then switching trains on their way to Randolph, where a gaggle of Dicky's friends awaited. He remembers staring up at Dicky, listening to his incessant, rambling chatter throughout those trips, and feeling an overwhelming sense of warmth, comfort, and safety.

By the time Micky reached his teens and started enjoying some amateur success of his own, Dicky[5] had become a Lowell legend. In fact, Ward had just turned 13 when he watched his 21-year-old big brother fight 10 rounds with then-undefeated future Hall of Famer Sugar Ray Leonard on national television in 1978.

As a role model, however, Dicky was tragically flawed. He dropped out of school as an eighth grader. Before he made it into his mid-20s, Dicky was addicted to crack cocaine, regarded as one of the most devastating of the street drugs. By the mid-1980s, his pro career was over and his name had gone from famous to infamous in Lowell. He had become well known to local police as a petty criminal, with regular arrests for drugs, drunkenness, strong-arm robberies, assault, and battery.

Through it all, he stayed in his younger brother's corner—literally—training Micky as an amateur and on into the professional ranks, to hopefully grow into the champion Dicky had failed to become. When he showed up at the gym, Dicky gave it everything he had. He did the roadwork with his brother. He served as Micky's sparring partner. He was a teacher, a strategist, a mentor. When he didn't show, those absences sometimes extended for days. There were occasions, in fact, when little brother marched boldly into Lowell's most dangerous crack houses in search of big brother.

It's anyone's guess how Micky's career might have been different if he'd given up on Dicky—which, from a boxing standpoint, certainly would have been justifiable. But Micky seems to have little doubt about the fate Dicky would have suffered if he had been tossed aside as Micky's trainer. They were family, literally blood brothers, which made Micky's love and loyalty unconditional.

Ward said his love for his brother never wavered, but he lived with a festering anger and resentment for what his brother was doing to himself, and to the family, with alcohol, drugs, and criminal activity, and the way he squandered what might have been a brilliant professional boxing career.

Ward also was bothered, often silently, by the occasions when Dicky wasn't around during his own career, not only in the gym, but occasionally on fight nights. He was equally disappointed on those days and nights when his brother arrived inebriated, or otherwise in a bad state, and was more of a nuisance than a help.

# 3

# ARTURO

**A**rturo Gatti was born in Cassino, Italy, in 1972—the same year Micky Ward first followed his big brother into Lowell's West End Gym—and moved to Montreal with his parents Ida and Giovanni as a toddler.

Giovanni Gatti was an electrician and a boxing fan, which, no doubt, is what drew his two sons to a boxing gym as children. Arturo was six years old the first time he wandered into a gym behind his 11-year-old brother Joe. He was eight when he had his first amateur fight. He was a cheerful, energetic, seize-the-day kind of kid in the gym, but rarely was he a serious student of the sport in those earliest days. He mostly came to play.

"He liked to come to the gym and work out, fool around with the boys, tease them," says Abraham Pervin, Canada's 1976 Olympic boxing coach, in *Arturo Gatti: The People's Champion*, a documentary produced by Concrete Cinema. "They used to chase him around the ring, but they couldn't catch him."[1]

"I just did it because it was a sport. I played soccer and hockey in Canada," Gatti told Evan Rothman of *New Jersey Monthly*. "It was fun, and knowing how to fight was great for me growing up because no bullies bugged me, and I was a small guy."[2]

Young Gatti attended a French school in the eclectic city of Montreal and grew up speaking French, Italian, and English. He was well liked by teachers and classmates, and achieved high marks, his mother said, even though Gatti, himself, would admit later that he had little interest in school. For Arturo, life was meant to be lived, even at a young age. He was a good little kid—happy, friendly, and mischievous, with a penchant for pranks.

"He wasn't the one who liked discipline the most," says trainer-turned-promoter Yvon Michel in a Canadian documentary. "He was talented. He was winning. But he had his own agenda. It was like, 'Ah, look, just have fun here. We enjoy life.'"[3]

Arturo was 15 when his father fell off a ladder at work and died. That's when Ida Gatti's younger son became more serious about boxing "to make his dad proud," she recalled.[4]

Gatti's family was related by marriage to a famous Canadian boxing clan, the Hiltons, and young Arturo honed his skills sparring with the brothers—Matthew (who won the IBF light middleweight crown in 1987), Davey (who became WBC super middleweight champion in 2000), and Jimmy (who had a two-fight pro career).

The teenaged Gatti was talented enough as an amateur to compile an 86–14 record and win three Canadian Golden Gloves championships and two national titles, but it was evident even then that his aggressive, hard-hitting style was better suited for the professional version of the sport, which is about inflicting damage, than the amateur game, which is geared toward scoring points. Gatti had dreams of representing Canada at the Olympic Games, but ran into a roadblock named Mike Strange, a 10-time Canadian champion who fought in three Olympics. After losing to Strange, Gatti shrugged off the rest of his amateur career and decided to turn pro at age 19.

Michel, who went on to become the top promoter in Canada, told him he was making the biggest mistake of his life. He later admitted he had been wrong.

In 1991, a teenaged Gatti moved to Jersey City, New Jersey, where his 24-year-old brother already was living, training, and fighting professionally. Joe Gatti was 13–2 by the time Arturo made his pro debut on June 10, 1991, at the Meadowlands Convention Center in Secaucus, New Jersey. Mark Breland won the main event that night, beating Henry Anaya by decision in 10 rounds. Joe fought Ralph Moncrief in the 10-round semi-main and came away with a majority-decision victory. Arturo's debut was the second bout of the evening, a scheduled four-rounder against a Trenton lightweight, Jose Gonzales.

"I looked across the room and saw him, and I was like, 'Oh, man . . .' I was scared to death," Gatti recounted. "Here was a guy fresh out of the can, with a ponytail and tattoos all over his body. I was a teenager. I never saw anything like him before in my life."[5]

Gonzales didn't make it to the final bell. Gatti stopped him in 1:27 of the third round with a left hook that would become his signature punch for the rest of his 16-year, 49-fight career.

Arturo Gatti was a brilliantly talented fighter from the beginning—exceptionally quick on his feet, with blazing hand speed, a big punch, and, of course, a chin like the Rock of Gibraltar. He was wildly popular with boxing fans, promoters, and the television networks because he invariably delivered a fight worth watching.

Boxing photographer Tom Casino met the 19-year-old boxer soon after Gatti moved to New Jersey, watched him fight, and was smitten immediately. "Arturo was special . . . there was nobody like him. He looked like this little peanut, but the guy couldn't hit him . . . and he's pot-shotting the guy, and then hitting him like *bang*," Casino says in *Legendary Nights: The Tale of Arturo Gatti vs. Micky Ward*, an HBO documentary. "He won and I was like, 'Wow, I've never seen anything like it.' I knew this guy was gonna be a champ."[6]

Like so many gifted fighters who came before him, it's only speculative how much he might have accomplished if he'd taken the sport more seriously from the beginning of his career through his glory years. Gatti's attraction to the party life in New Jersey and New York was (and is) part of his legend and legacy. Casino says Gatti played at least as hard as he worked in the early days of his professional career. He drank. He dabbled in recreational drugs. He chased women. He fought in parking lots. He drove fast. Casino remembers getting regular phone calls from someone telling him that Arturo had done "something crazy." Relates Casino, "Everybody I met in the tristate area had a party story about Arturo Gatti."

It's not hard to understand why. Gatti was a single man with matinee-idol looks; a chiseled physique; a vibrant, outgoing personality; a great sense of humor; and a smile so luminescent that it might have been visible from space. His machismo was legendary in the ring, and the vast majority of those who met him regarded him as a great guy outside the ring. He was friendly and approachable to almost anyone who saw him on the street or in a bar. Toss in the celebrity factor—Gatti quickly became a headliner on ESPN, the USA Network, and later HBO—and you've got a package that was catnip to beautiful women. What kind of man can stay dedicated, under those circumstances, to the monkish lifestyle that professional boxing demands?

"I've known quite a number of fighters who could party really hard. I've spent some very long, entertaining evenings with fighters who were pushing themselves to the limit in that regard, the same way they would push themselves to the limit in the ring," states HBO's Jim Lampley. "And there was nobody like Arturo."[7]

"My wife and I would always worry, if the phone rang at three in the morning, hoping it was just him asking to extend the credit card, or asking for a few dollars, hoping he wasn't in trouble," comments Gatti's manager, Pat Lynch, in *Legendary Nights*.

"He partied like he fought—hard and heavy," Casino says.

A trait shared by the vast majority of professional fighters who are young, talented, and undefeated is the delusion of invincibility. The fact that they've never failed to conquer is evidence, at least to them, that they cannot lose—that they'll always find a way to prevail. What they choose to ignore is the history that has been written by virtually every boxer who ever lived—each of whom, perhaps partially out of necessity, carried the same self-belief, right up until the moment when, to their own astonishment, they discovered that they were not, in fact, 10 feet tall and bulletproof.

The reality that is conveniently compartmentalized by every undefeated fighter is that the man in the opposite corner oftentimes is brimming with his own confidence, adorned with his own dangerous skills, and, in some cases, is better prepared. He trained longer and harder. He ran farther, studied fight films more intensely, listened more carefully to his trainers and strategists, and—maybe most important of all—showed up on fight night with more hunger in his gut. A fighter who doesn't believe he can lose is ripe for the picking, and the structure of professional boxing—the more you win, the tougher the competition gets—is a built-in recipe for that inevitable failure. A hard fall is all but guaranteed at some point.

The lure of the nightlife can be irresistible to an attractive, young, celebrity boxer, who, in most cases, comes from meager beginnings, a broken family, mean streets and has a craving for any kind of relevance. And then, all of a sudden, it happens, all of it, on one magical night. He faces somebody with a bigger reputation, knocks him off, and grabs a headline in the morning paper, and, virtually overnight, he is somebody.

"A lot of guys are tortured, man . . . they live a lifestyle," Hall of Famer Ray "Boom Boom" Mancini comments. "I don't know if it's them or how they think they're expected to act, but they all want that rock star life."[8]

What is usually impossible for the fighter to grasp as a young superstar is the subtle evaporation of the hunger that drove him to the top in the first place. That almost-imperceptible deterioration of work ethic and determination often is the difference between staying at the top and taking a startling tumble at the hands of a hungrier, more-focused opponent.

There's little evidence to indicate that Arturo Gatti was tortured or troubled as a young man. More likely, he simply drank up the rock star life and had an unwavering (if misguided) faith and belief that his raw talent and fight-night determination would get him past anyone a promoter chose to put in front of him.

"Fighting with no gloves would have been right up Arturo's alley," said former trainer Buddy McGirt. "With padding, he broke his hands five times. Without it, his hands would still be broke."[9]

Gatti knocked out the first five men he faced—four in the opening seconds—and won a pair of six-round decisions before a Philadelphia tough guy who went by the name King Solomon put a blemish on his record. Fighting at the historic Blue Horizon, his home arena, Solomon outpointed Gatti on two of three scorecards.

But, by nature, Arturo was not a worried man—an attitude he relentlessly validated with 23 straight wins, 18 by knockout. One attention-getter in that string was a first-round technical knockout of former WBF featherweight champion Pete Taliaferro (25–2 at the time) in June 1994—a victory that made Gatti the USBA super featherweight belt-holder.

Eighteen months and seven fights later, the 23-year-old Gatti (23–1, 20 KOs) found himself on HBO at the "Mecca of Boxing," Madison Square Garden, with a shot at the IBF super featherweight championship, held by Tracy Harris Patterson (adopted son of two-time world heavyweight king Floyd Patterson), who was 54–3–1, with 39 KOs. Gatti arrived with a slugger's reputation, with Patterson in the boxer's role. It was the first boxing event in two and a half years at the Garden.

If Gatti had compromised his training with wine, women, and song, it wasn't immediately evident that night against Patterson. An uppercut put the defending champion on the canvas midway through the second round—only the third knockdown of his 58-fight career. An unexpected strategy—the slugger jabbed incessantly, setting up sizzling combinations—created another puzzle for Patterson, who had the prefight reputation as the slicker of the two.

HBO analyst Larry Merchant and "unofficial ringside scorer" Harold Lederman, a Hall of Fame boxing judge, gave six of the first seven rounds to Gatti.

"He's handling the situation beautifully," Merchant said during round 9. "He looks like an old-fashioned Garden fighter."

Coming from Merchant, a native New Yorker and journalism legend, no compliment could have been greater.

"There have been many outstanding Italians who have fought at the Garden—LaMotta, Marciano, Graziano—and it looks like we may have another champion," he added a round later.

By the end of the round, Gatti began slugging with Patterson—a harbinger of the style that would make him famous and beloved. He was content to exchange big shots, despite a badly swollen and bleeding left eye, which hindered his radar for Patterson's right hand. By the end of the 11th, Gatti's right eye also was swelling shut. The last two rounds were among Patterson's best of the fight—Gatti couldn't see, and, for whatever reason, his legs were gone—but he fought hard to the final bell. All three judges scored the fight for the sport's newest meteorite.

At 23, Gatti was a world champion, and, as it turned out, his remarkable story was merely in its infancy.

# 4

# BROTHER'S KEEPER

**W**hen Micky Ward won New England's Silver Mittens championship at age 14, he weighed 90 pounds. A few months later, after a 10-pound growth spurt, he became the region's Junior Olympic champ. The following year, at 15, he captured his first New England Golden Gloves crown in the 112-pound division, and at 16, the 5-foot-5 Ward took the 125-pound title.

After losing in the 132-pound finals at 17, Ward moved to the 140-pound weight class, which would be his home for the remainder of his career. By that time, he stood 5-foot-8, and his best assets were lightning-quick hands and a natural quickness in the ring. Building on those traits, he fancied himself more of a boxer than a puncher, learning how to hit and move—abilities amateur boxing judges love.

That early incarnation of Ward will surprise fans who followed his professional career—particularly his later years—when he had become a prototypical brawler who preferred to stand forehead-to-forehead with an opponent, banging incessantly to the body and head while constantly pushing forward. The other trait that endeared Ward to fans during his professional glory years was a mule-stubborn willingness to absorb punishment.

Ward generally had a realistic opinion of his own strengths and weaknesses, a unique trait in a fighter. Too often, fighters are delusional about their own abilities, believing they're better boxers, punchers, or defenders than they really are. In Ward's case, he came to realize that his style wasn't necessarily conducive to amateur boxing, which awards a point to a fighter for every "touch" during a match. A soft jab counts the same as a knockdown in the amateur ranks.

He understood at a young age that he wasn't going to outbox a true boxer, but his left hook to the body could cave in an opponent's ribcage. If there was any doubt about that, affirmation came when Ward made his pro debut on June 13, 1985, in front of a few hundred fans at a roller-skating rink in nearby Lawrence, Massachusetts. His opponent, David Morin, felt his ribs break when Ward landed the body shot just two minutes into the fight, and, just like that, the freshly minted pro from Lowell was 1–0, with one KO.

Another attribute was that Ward was, for the most part, a good listener. He trusted the man giving him advice between rounds—his brother Dicky—who understood from his own experiences that if you batter your opponent's body, his hands will drop and his head will be exposed. Working the torso also drains an opponent's stamina and takes away any mobility as a fight wears on.

The formula worked for Ward's first 14 fights, 10 of which ended early. But success in boxing doesn't happen on fight night as much as in the weeks and months leading up to the opening bell. Many a promising boxer has fallen prey to an inadequate infrastructure—inept management, lackadaisical training habits, poor diet, distractions, or any number of other potential pitfalls.

The greatest threat to Ward's career, particularly in the early days, was his beloved hometown. Drinking heavily was an accepted way of life in Lowell. Cocaine was readily available to anyone with a taste. The gutters were littered with people who had thrown their lives away on booze, coke, heroin, methamphetamine, prostitution and street hustlers, and other temptations. Meanwhile, like a notorious gunfighter drinking in a Wild West saloon, Ward was rarely very far away from some intoxicated bad-ass who viewed the celebrated boxer as a way to boost his own street cred.

Friends remember Ward as a mostly levelheaded partier who usually went to great lengths to avoid a scrap, particularly after he started getting paid to fight in the ring. But in Lowell, there was someone on every corner who wouldn't accept "We're not lookin' for any trouble" as an out. Too often, one thing led to another, and fists were flying. And even if Ward was able to talk his way out of a fight, his rough-and-tumble friends often didn't bother to try. If a pal was getting hammered in an unfair fight, it was an indelible part of the code of the streets that Ward would jump in.

Friends say he busted up his hands numerous times throughout the years in street fights, but the incident generally credited for having the greatest long-term effect on his career happened in the spring of 1987, at the infamous Cosmopolitan Cafe, on Market Street, a place that seemed to attract every troublemaker in Lowell, particularly around closing time.

The lives of Micky Ward and his brother Dicky Eklund were on starkly different trajectories in the spring of 1987.

Micky was 21 years old, and his boxing career was on a roll. Less than two years after his pro debut he was 13–0, with nine knockouts, including a fourth-round TKO of Kelly Koble in the famous outdoor arena at Caesars Palace—his first Las Vegas fight—on the undercard of the Sugar Ray Leonard–Marvelous Marvin Hagler event.

At that point of his life and career, Ward was feeling good.

One of the few drawbacks was the constant whirlwind of chaos that always seemed to blow through the door with his brother Dicky, who by then was beginning to run into serious trouble on a regular basis, often running afoul of local law enforcement. He was, most likely, a full-blown crack addict by then, and his circle of friends—wide and diverse—included many reckless rogues who always seemed to be doing the wrong thing in the wrong place at the wrong time.

On May 9, 1987, a Saturday night, Micky and a group of friends went bar hopping in Lowell, where, as closing time approached, all roads always seemed to lead to the notorious Cosmopolitan Cafe on Market Street. By Ward's own account, the Cosmo was a place that was best to avoid, a den of iniquity where people snorted coke off the bathroom sinks and drank until their best judgment—if they'd started the night with any—had been obliterated.

It was already 1 a.m. when Ward's crowd arrived at the Cosmo—their final stop—walking through the gauntlet of motorcycles parked outside. Trouble started only a short time later, when Ward's friend, Mike Lapoint, spotted a man who had dated his mother, a relationship that allegedly had become physically abusive. Lapoint, says Ward, wasn't one to let bygones be bygones, especially after he'd been drinking for most of an evening, as he had been on this night when he walked up and confronted the ex-boyfriend in the crowded bar. After a heated face-to-face, the two were headed to the parking lot, with an entourage of equally intoxicated barflies in tow. That crowd included Dicky Eklund and some of his friends. The fight commenced, with Lapoint—bigger, stronger, younger—getting the best of his adversary. He knocked his opponent to the pavement, jumped on top of him, and beat him ruthlessly until Dicky intervened, yelling, "C'mon, that's enough! He's a friend of mine!"

Ward doubts that his brother's friendship with the victim was very deep—if it existed at all—but says Dicky knew almost everyone in Lowell, so he doesn't doubt that they were acquainted.

As police cars skidded to a halt outside the bar, sirens wailing, Lapoint did the intelligent thing and fled, disappearing into the night via a nearby canal path. One of the 13 responding officers, Edward Dowling, filed an incident report that said Dicky was punching and kicking 29-year-old Angel Rosaria when they arrived. But by Ward's account in his autobiography, *A Warrior's Heart*, police got there just in time to see Dicky—the well-known troublemaker—pulling the bloodied loser to his feet and made the assumption that seemed logical. Ward says he can still see the look in Dicky's eyes as the police charged him, wielding nightsticks.[1]

Ward watched his brother scuffle with police, who cuffed his hands behind his back and threw him face-first onto the ground. At that moment, the little brother—himself buzzed by alcohol—launched himself into the fray. In Ward's estimation, Dicky was being wrongly accused—for once—and was undeserving of the beating he was taking from the Lowell Police Department. If family blood was to be spilled, he felt a loyalty to add his to the mix.

Bad idea. He immediately felt the sting of a large police flashlight against his ribcage. Then he was clubbed again, this time on the side of the head. By Ward's account, he was hit multiple times on the head, body, and hands, even after he had been handcuffed and subdued.

Ward's cousin, Mike Lutkus, offered a slightly different account, saying Micky tackled a cop, forcing him to the ground, and another man kicked the officer while he was down. That, he said, is when the army in blue descended upon Micky with full force. As he lay on the ground, Ward says he heard someone in the crowd yell, "Hey, don't you know who that is? It's Micky Ward!"

"Fuck Micky Ward!" a cop shouted, according to Lutkus. "Then another one says, 'Break his hands so he can't fight again!' And they cracked him again."[2]

Ward's account in *A Warrior's Heart* is that police struck his hands multiple times as he was handcuffed on the ground. The last few blows— "three or four" to his hands and arms—did the most damage. As police were slamming the paddy wagon doors on Ward and Eklund, their sister Gail—aka "Red Dog"—joined the fracas, demanding to be arrested along with her brothers. The police were happy to accommodate. Two Eklunds and one Ward were shackled side-by-side in the police wagon, drunk, raging, and spouting blood. Dicky and Gail were hauled to the precinct and formally booked. Micky was taken to a hospital, where he took six stitches to the head and underwent multiple X-rays.

After he had been pieced back together, Ward was sent home to sleep it off, but the damage that had been done, particularly to his hands, would haunt him throughout his professional boxing career.

# 5

# ROLLER COASTER

**A**rturo Gatti's journey to the trilogy that would cement his legacy as a boxing legend was completely different from the path Micky Ward would take.

Gatti became the IBF super featherweight champion of the world when he was just 23 years old, taking the title from Tracy Harris Patterson at Madison Square Garden in 1995.

He was back in the ring just three months later to defend the belt against Wilson Rodriguez, a rough, 30-year-old Dominican whose evolution in the sport had mostly been rudderless, particularly in his early days as a pro. In his first five years as a prizefighter, Rodriguez fought 25 times, and his record was blemished with five losses and three draws, almost entirely against obscure fighters. But by the time he got in the ring with Gatti, he had turned his career around in a big way. After losing an eight-round decision in December 1990, to an undefeated Jimmi Bredahl (a future two-division world champion), Rodriguez went on a 27–1 run. The only loss during that five-year span happened in an IBF super featherweight title fight against defending champ John John Molina, who knocked him out in the 10th round. Rodriguez responded to that setback with another five-fight winning streak (four of those wins by KO) to earn a shot at Gatti, who, by then, held the same belt that had been vacated by Molina, who had moved up in weight.

Gatti met Rodriguez in Madison Square Garden on March 23, 1996, knocking him out in the sixth round of a fight that was so pyrotechnic that it was named by *Ring* magazine as a runner-up for "Fight of the Year" honors to Evander Holyfield's upset of Mike Tyson.

By the end of the opening round against Rodriguez, both of Gatti's eyes already were badly swollen. Rodriguez decked Gatti in round 2, which Gatti identified as an epiphany, not only in the fight, but also in his career.

"When I got dropped . . . I never believed I could ever get dropped, but I guess I can," he said. "I got scared when I went down, and I didn't even know I was down until I looked around and said, 'Oh, my god . . . I'm going to lose the fight.'" [1]

Gatti turned the momentum in round 5, crumpling the Dominican to the canvas with a left hook that broke one of Rodriguez's ribs. In the sixth round, Gatti, nearly blind from the grotesque swelling, landed another vicious hook on the same splintered rib. That sent Rodriguez to the canvas for the second and final time, and Gatti retained his title.

Two fights later, in February 1997, he outpointed Patterson for the second time. The following May, he won a seven-round technical decision at Caesars Palace in Atlantic City over former IBF featherweight champ Calvin Grove, who, by then, was well over the hill.

What happened next, when combined with the Wilson Rodriguez spectacle, would cement Gatti's claim to a nickname that would follow him throughout the rest of his career: the "Human Highlight Reel."

In October 1997, he returned to Caesars Palace for his third title defense, against former WBC super featherweight king Gabriel Ruelas, a Mexican hooker/body-puncher who had won his belt from rugged Jesse James Leija. Between his conquest of Leija and the loss of his championship to Azumah Nelson the following December, Ruelas had knocked out Jimmy Garcia, a 23-year-old Colombian, in Las Vegas. Garcia died after the fight, a tragedy that would haunt Ruelas during the Nelson bout, just seven months later, and for the rest of his career. But whatever he had left, he saved for Gatti. Both fighters suffered mightily to make the 130-pound weight limit for their title bout and were visibly gaunt at the weigh-in. Both rehydrated dramatically overnight: HBO's unofficial weigh-in on fight night showed Ruelas had gained 15 pounds and Gatti 15 1/2.

They battered one another in Atlantic City for three rough rounds before Gatti's soon-to-be-legendary heart and will came into play. In the fourth round, Ruelas (44–3, 23 KOs) hurt the champion badly and reeled off a string of 17 unanswered punches, beginning with a mammoth left uppercut with less than a minute left, followed immediately by a hard right to Gatti's beltline. How Gatti made it to the bell that round became part of his enduring lore. He not only persevered, but also inexplicably landed a few big shots of his own just before the end of the round.

The fifth round—the most violent of the fight—began with a fierce, minute-long exchange, from which Gatti emerged with a nasty cut under his already-swollen left eye. The brutality continued until Gatti caught an advancing Ruelas with two right hands and then a monstrous left hook to the head that abruptly dropped the 27-year-old ex-champ. Ruelas struggled to his feet at the count of eight, but staggered away from referee Benji Esteves Jr., who immediately waved his arms to stop the fight. The official time was 2:22.

"Arturo Gatti was one of the hardest punchers I ever fought. I think only Azumah Nelson hit harder," Ruelas said later. "Gatti gave me my toughest fight."

Ruelas added,

> Arturo was someone that I really liked. I liked how he fought, I liked how he came to fight. At that time he didn't box a lot; he just came out and traded punches, which is what I liked doing. That was great. I didn't have to chase him in the ring.
>
> Plus he had a name, he had a lot of media, he had a following. I thought, what could be better than to go beat him in his own house, which was Atlantic City. I think it was a great fight, and, of course, I felt like it was stopped too soon. But I also thought, oh, well, I'll get him in the rematch. But I never got it.[2]

Gatti's sensational victory was honored as *Ring* magazine's "Fight of the Year" for 1997, and the "Human Highlight Reel" had solidified his reputation as a golden goose for the HBO television network. Indeed, he was also instrumental in convincing the worldwide boxing community that the lightweight divisions are truly where the action is.

The Ruelas fight would be Gatti's finale at 130 pounds. It would also be his last victory in nearly two years.

Angel Manfredy called himself "El Diablo" and wore a latex Satan mask during his ring walks as homage to his wild life outside of the ring—binges of booze and cocaine that ended only after he nearly committed suicide one night on the tail end of a three-day bender. That's when Manfredy says he heard the voice of God telling him to clean up his life.

The devil mask was gone, but the "El Diablo" moniker was still on the back of his robe and part of Michael Buffer's prefight introduction on January 17, 1998, when Manfredy met Arturo Gatti on HBO for a 10-round nontitle bout at Convention Hall in Atlantic City. Just before taking final instructions at ring center, he looked toward the heavens and appeared to whisper a short prayer. A tattoo of a naked lady on his left shoulder was now accompanied by a cross. He had worked hard to become a different man and was determined to demonstrate to a worldwide television audience that he also was a more dedicated fighter.

Not that the earlier version of Manfredy had been run-of-the-mill.

He was of Puerto Rican descent, the son of a steelworker in Gary, Indiana, where kids grew up tough. He fought 56 times as an amateur, winning 48, and turned pro in June 1993, against Charles McClellan, who stopped Manfredy in the second round. His second pro fight against Jose Luis Carrillo ended in a draw, and he lost again in his fifth outing to Jeff Mason. None of those opponents made so much as a ripple in the rest of their own pro careers.

Evidence was abundant that Manfredy had chosen the wrong sport, but boxers are often adroit at dismissing rational thought. From there, Manfredy embarked on a four-year, 21-fight winning streak. It included conquests of fading fringe contenders Harold Petty, Wilfredo Ruiz, and Wilson Rodriguez; former belt-holder Calvin Grove; and, most recently, an eighth-round TKO victory over Jorge Paez for the WBU super featherweight crown. Gatti had everything Manfredy wanted. He held the IBF super featherweight championship. He could pack any arena and draw huge television audiences to HBO. And, as a result, his paydays had made him a wealthy man.

"About three years earlier, my wife and I were watching ESPN2 on TV and Gatti was the main event," Manfredy said.

> He knocked this dude out—just a nasty KO—and I remember pointing to the TV and saying, "I'm going to fight that guy one day." My wife just laughed and said, "Yeah . . . right." And at that moment, in my mind and in my soul, I was thinking, "We'll see about that." I like to hear that kind of doubt. It motivates me.[3]

Although Gatti and Manfredy each held their own version of the 130-pound title, no belts were on the line because this one would take place at 135 pounds, the first time either fighter had ventured into the lightweight division. The sports books in Atlantic City, where Gatti had been adopted as a hometown fighter, made "El Diablo" a big underdog, but boxing's oracles expected nothing but fireworks. Gatti (29–1, 24 KOs) was, after all, the "Human Highlight Reel," and Manfredy (22–2–1, 18 KOs) had earned a reputation as a hard-hitting warrior with a granite chin. HBO's TV crew—Jim Lampley, Larry Merchant, and George Foreman—gave Manfredy the edge in quickness and boxing skills.

"I didn't fight him for money. I didn't fight him for a belt. I took the fight for the name: Arturo Gatti," Manfredy told the authors of this book. "He was one of the best-known fighters in the world at the time, and higher-rated than me, and the fight was going to be seen all over the world on HBO. I was very determined to beat him, and I gave one of the best performances of my career."

Manfredy was, in fact, brilliant that night, and Gatti was Gatti—ferocious and relentless. They would bludgeon one another for eight sensational rounds. As it turned out, the pivotal moment of the fight occurred with less than 10 seconds left in the opening round, when "El Diablo" slashed open Gatti's left eyelid with a quick, straight, lead right hand. In Gatti's favor, one of the greatest cutmen in boxing history, Joe Souza, was waiting in the corner when the bell rang, but the TV cameras told the story: The gash was wide, deep, and nasty, and Souza clearly was going to need everything in his legendary tool kit to stop the blood flow.

Gatti had won the first round with aggression, heavy body shots, and quick combinations, but Manfredy was more effective in round 2, landing 24 of 37 power punches and reopening the cut. At 1:05 of the third round, he spun Gatti to the canvas with a sizzling left hook to the jaw.

"He's hurt . . . he's hurt badly . . . otherwise he wouldn't have gotten up so quickly," Merchant observed on the HBO broadcast, as Gatti instinctively wobbled to his feet at the count of four. Indeed, veteran boxers in total command of their faculties will usually stay down for at least a seven- or eight-count, taking advantage of every precious second of recovery time. If a fighter bounces up immediately from a bad knockdown, it's often a sign that he's letting instinct overrule his ring intellect.

"Hard to imagine Gatti coming back from this," Lampley added.

But, as the broadcast team knew well, Gatti's greatness stemmed from his otherworldly ability to defy any boxing fan's imagination by fighting through impossible waves of adversity. Less than 15 seconds later, he was hammering Manfredy with both hands—hard, loud punches that had a thunderstruck Lampley screaming into the mic. When the bell sounded, Gatti glanced over his shoulder and grinned at his opponent as he walked toward his corner. Meanwhile, a waterfall of blood rolled down his face.

"A boxer's greatest fear in the dressing room before a fight is, 'I do not want to get hurt,'" offered Foreman. "Gatti doesn't have those feelings. He anticipates getting hurt."

Rounds 4, 5, and 6 were scintillating. When Manfredy boxed and controlled the space, he scored points and created opportunities for himself to land huge shots on Gatti, who couldn't see many of the punches coming through the blood flowing into his left eye. At close quarters, Gatti assaulted "El Diablo's" ribcage (rumored to have been injured three weeks before the fight) and spun Manfredy's head with three- and four-punch combinations. When the bell sounded to end the seventh round, the ring doctor followed Gatti to his corner and examined the gory cave in his left eyelid. The physician turned to referee Wayne Hedgepeth, as heard on the HBO telecast, and said, "You can keep it going as long as he keeps defending himself and throwing punches."

Gatti did exactly that throughout round 8, pressuring Manfredy aggressively but absorbing as much punishment as he gave. Gatti's face was a crimson mask at the bell, and the fight was stopped. The loser didn't protest.

One judge had the fight scored even. The other two had Manfredy on top.

Gatti said afterward that he wanted a rematch. Manfredy said he wanted to return to 130 pounds to fight British superstar Prince Naseem Hamed. Neither fighter would get his wish. Manfredy, who dropped the "El Diablo" moniker in favor of a new one—"Got Jesus?"—went on to fight a nondescript journeyman, Isander Lacen (12–8–4), in his next bout. Next up for the "Human Highlight Reel" would be a Philadelphia gladiator named Ivan Robinson—and, unbelievably, yet another *Ring* magazine "Fight of the Year."

Like soldiers who survive the battlefield, professional boxers almost literally become blood brothers, developing a depth of respect that cannot be shared or fully understood by anyone else. That's why two archrival fighters invariably embrace and whisper into one another's ears after spending the preceding 45 minutes battering one another into tender sirloin. Few moments outside of sexual intimacy are comparable. Call it intimate warfare.

Ivan Robinson and Arturo Gatti were friends before and after they became foes. Both had trained regularly, often side-by-side, with one of the greatest fighters of their era—of any era—Pernell "Sweet Pea" Whitaker, who, by 1998, had eight world title belts in three weight divisions. At one point, Whitaker had been anointed number one in the world, pound-for-pound, by *Ring* magazine.

"Every time Pernell was getting ready for a big fight, it was always me and Arturo Gatti in camp with him," Robinson said. "But me and Arturo never sparred each other . . . we always just sparred with Pernell Whitaker."[4]

Robinson and Gatti became buddies outside the ropes, even outside the gym. They hung together and partied together. Neither gave a second thought to the possibility that they might someday have to fight one another. Likewise, neither hesitated at facing his friend in the ring for money in August 1998. From the opening bell to the final blow, boxing is literally a life-and-death struggle for the combatants. Before and after the fight, it's rarely personal.

"Me and Gatti formed a great friendship, a great relationship, but at the end of the day boxing is a business," Robinson said. "And anybody who knew Arturo would tell you the same thing: He didn't look at it as a friendship, he looked at it as business."

Nevertheless, Robinson was surprised when the fight was proposed and equally surprised that Gatti gave his blessing to his promoter, Kathy Duva of Main Events, to make it happen.

The Philadelphia fighter, who called himself "Mighty Ivan," had been nothing but authentic, a guy who could be counted on to give his all, every time he stepped into the ring, during a professional career that had been christened six years earlier and began with 23 consecutive victories. In December 1996, Robinson got his first shot at a world title—the IBF lightweight crown, held by Philip Holiday, who was 29–0—losing a hard-fought unanimous decision. Seven months later, he was back in the ring against Israel Cardona, a former two-division world champion who was coming off a narrow loss of his own against Charles Murray. Cardona dealt Robinson his second loss, a third-round technical knockout, from which "Mighty Ivan" rebounded with back-to-back victories to improve to 25–2.

Even though he and Gatti—then 29–2—shared a similar trajectory on paper, Robinson's appeal to fans, promoters, and television networks couldn't compare to that of the "Human Highlight Reel." Only serious fight fans recognized his name.

"I don't know what it was, but at that time nobody wanted to fight me. I could never get a shot at the title," he said.

> But, you know what? Arturo Gatti stuck his neck out and gave Ivan Robinson two chances to blossom. He birthed me. He brought me to life.
>
> He gave me what turned out to be the two biggest fights of my career, and to this day I've still got guys talking to me about it—new fighters, old fighters, fans . . . they're still talking about the Arturo Gatti fights. I guess I can go to my grave with that, and I've got to love Arturo Gatti for that.

By the time he stepped through the ropes at Convention Hall in Atlantic City to fight Robinson, Gatti was only seven months removed from his TKO loss to Manfredy at the same venue. That one had ended his six-year, 23-fight winning streak. No doubt, the loss to Manfredy had hurt his career—no sport punishes failure as heartlessly as boxing—but Arturo was still a main-event attraction for HBO. In 1996, there was no greater validation of a fighter's relevance than HBO's unconditional love. At the same time, Gatti understood that another setback was probably a ticket to the sport's minor leagues—particularly if it came at the hands of an opponent who was somewhere on the periphery of stardom. The stakes were high, and so was the risk: Gatti knew his friend was no chump.

The Atlantic City fight crowd regarded Gatti as a hometown fighter, an adopted son. He was, after all, a resident of Jersey City, two hours north of the Boardwalk. But Robinson was from Philly—just 60 miles away—and brought a significant fan base of his own to watch what ultimately became *Ring* magazine's 1998 "Fight of the Year."

The bookmakers made Robinson a 4–1 underdog. His own handlers also had their doubts. "My team thought it was going to be a great fight, but I don't think they believed I could beat him," Robinson said. "Gatti didn't think I could beat him, either, but I proved everybody wrong that night."

Gatti, by then, was celebrated for vaporizing opponents with his vaunted left hook, rescuing victories when he was behind on all score-cards. Robinson, by contrast, was a boxer, not a puncher. He had just 10 knockouts on his 25–2 record. "Mighty Ivan" had the quicker feet, the quicker hands, the longer reach by two inches, and, by most accounts, the superior boxing skills. And, as the underdog, he had little to lose and much to gain.

"Gatti's career was starting to die out a little bit at the time because he had just lost to Manfredy. His stock had kind of gone down," Robinson recollected. "I needed to get into a good fight, and that's what the Arturo Gatti fight was about. I turned down nobody, so why would I turn down Arturo Gatti? I mean, even though he had lost to Manfredy, Arturo Gatti was still one of the hot fighters in the world."

Robinson declared afterward that he had been the hungrier fighter that night. He also had what turned out to be a surprisingly effective game plan, showing a level of fearlessness and aggression from the opening bell that probably surprised Gatti. By the end of three action-packed rounds, Gatti was cut and swelling under the left eye. But if Robinson had momentum, it went away with 43 seconds left in round 4. That's when Gatti landed what replays showed to be a glancing blow to his opponent's temple, which, coupled with a tangle of feet, sent "Mighty Ivan" tumbling to the canvas. Robinson rose quickly, unhurt, and engaged in a furious exchange until the bell sounded.

A bigger moment for Gatti came with 20 seconds left in the sixth, when he landed a bomb that sent his opponent stumbling backward, in such trouble that referee Earl Morton stared into Robinson's eyes, look-ing for signs of vacancy. The pro-Gatti crowd was on its feet at the bell. Both corners knew the outcome was up for grabs going into the 10th and final round. Robinson's hustle gave him the edge until the 44-second mark, when Gatti—as he was known to do—landed a mammoth hook to the forehead. Robinson fell hard against the ropes before righting himself and then endured Gatti's furious attempt to finish him off.

Ringside judge Ed Leahy scored the fight to Gatti, 96–93. Melvina Lathan and Steve Weisfeld saw it for Robinson, 98–93 and 96–94, re-spectively. Predictably, the two buddies fell into a warm embrace when the decision was announced. The 10-round fireworks show not only won

"Fight of the Year" honors, but also was judged by *Ring* magazine to be 1998's "Upset of the Year."

"Ivan Robinson was a great fighter and a hard style for me to fight against," Gatti recalls in the documentary *Arturo Gatti: The People's Champion*. " But those also were the years when . . . you know, I was going nuts in those years. I was making money. I was going out. I was just having a good time. When you're doing that stuff, you can't achieve what you want, you can't perform the way you're supposed to."

Four months later, across town at the Trump Taj Mahal, they did it again, waging another sensational war. Robinson won again, this time by unanimous decision, but two of the three judges saw it as a one-point fight—significant, since Gatti had been penalized a point for low blows during round 8. Without the deduction, those scorecards would have been even, resulting in a majority draw. But that's boxing. One fighter's career moment invariably becomes his opponent's heartbreak. It is a sport derived from the survival-of-the-fittest law that presides over even the highest level of the animal kingdom. Arturo Gatti, a world champion only a year earlier, entered 1999 on a three-fight losing streak, wondering if his career would ever really matter again.

"Boxing is a business that is done with us before we realize it, when we are replaced by men younger and stronger and faster who can make more money for the people who run it," said Hall of Famer Sugar Ray Leonard.[5]

And if a fighter's career no longer matters to fans, promoters, matchmakers, and television networks, it usually stops mattering to the fighter.

# 6

# BLOOD IS NOT ALWAYS THICKER

**D**icky Eklund and his sister Gail—better known in the neighborhood as "Red Dog"—became overnight guests of the Lowell, Massachusetts, police department the night of the parking lot brawl at the Cosmo. Their brother, Micky Ward, was taken to the hospital to have the flesh on his bleeding scalp reassembled and X-rays on his right hand, both of which had been waylaid by police nightsticks. What doctors found in the hand was a "hairline fracture," a diagnosis that almost seemed to amuse Ward years later:

> Funny thing about that term—*hairline fracture*. It sounds so innocuous, as if the injury isn't all that severe. Tiny, narrow. Easy to fix. In reality, though, a hairline fracture can be worse than a clean break. With a clean break there's a standard protocol for recovery and rehabilitation. With a hairline fracture, everything is kind of murky and unsettled. You think you're better when you really aren't. The pain starts to subside, the range of motion returns, so you get back in the gym and start working the bag, maybe sparring a little. Then, all of a sudden . . . crack! It happens all over again.[1]

Ward says he fought with a badly damaged right hand—pain, swelling, and degenerative bone disease—for 12 years after the Cosmo incident. But boxers are a different breed. Pain and discomfort are a part of everyday life for them, usually from childhood onward. The mentality, nurtured from their earliest days in the gym, is to ignore pain, blood, dizziness, or any other malady and keep moving forward. Acknowledging pain is tantamount to acknowledging weakness, and a fighter's very survival depends on showing no weakness.

So Ward trained on, hammering the heavy bag, the mitts, the speed bag, and his sparring partners every day, plunging his throbbing hands into a bucket of ice afterward. Ward says it simply became a normal and acceptable part of his routine.

Ward took his 13–0 record back into the ring less than four months after the Cosmo brawl, stopping Derrick McGuire, a 13–4 opponent, in the fourth round of a fight in Atlantic City. A month later, he went back to fight Edwin Curet, whose 21–7–2 record included losses to Livingstone Bramble and Greg Haugen. Curet was, in boxing parlance, a stepping-stone opponent, a graduation exam, for a young, unbeaten prospect.

Curet was smart, experienced, and durable. Ward was essentially a one-handed fighter, suffering with pain and swelling throughout training camp and unable to generate any power with his right hand during the fight. A 10-round split decision went to Curet, who tagged Ward with the first quantifiable setback of his pro career. According to Ward, suffering that first professional loss is akin to losing one's virginity. You'll never be unblemished again. For a boxer, he says, it is a rite of passage.

Gone, too, is the fighter's own mindset of invincibility. Suddenly, he has a chink in his armor that wasn't there before. He is forced to relinquish the delusion that he is unbeatable—that no matter what the circumstances, no matter who the opponent, he will always find a way to overcome and prevail. Now, somewhere in the rational portion of his mind, he knows better. He will always know better. Promoters and television networks also are infamously unsympathetic to losers. A record that is blemished just once in 14 fights won't turn the fighter into a nonentity, but an unspoken probationary period descends like a threatening storm cloud. The ledge overlooking oblivion becomes a bit more precarious, feeling like it could crumble beneath the fighter's feet at any moment.

Coming from a boxing family, and a boxing community, Ward knew the game. Another loss to another "stepping-stone" could make Ward, himself, into a mere stepping-stone for other more worthy up-and-comers. The only reasonable strategy, he decided, was to get back into the gym as soon as possible and win the next one.

He brought his damaged right hand back to Atlantic City three months later to fight Joey "Bugsy" Ferrell, a Philadelphia product who was 7–7–2. Realizing that the injury would worsen as the fight progressed,

Ward embraced the prefight strategy recommended by his brother, Dicky: "Jump all over him." He took Ferrell's breath away with a clean left to the ribcage in the opening seconds and then unloaded every punch in his arsenal until referee Vince Rainone intervened. The official time of the stoppage was 2:36.

During the next six months, he won three more—10-round decisions over Joey Olivera, who was 20–12–1, and David Silva, who was 1–7, followed by a first-round KO of Marvin Garris, 14–8–1. Although none of those three was, by itself, a career-booster, the winning streak lifted Ward to 17–1 and put him back onto the periphery of "contender" status, and into the conversation as a possible opponent for the better light welterweights in the world. He was offered the chance to fight former 140-pound king Saoul Mamby, who, by then, was also trying to climb the mountain all over again.

Ward versus Mamby was scheduled for September in Atlantic City, but Mamby came down with a virus that took him out of the fight, and Top Rank matchmaker Ron Katz found a last-minute substitute. Mike Mungin was 17–2 and once had a reputation as a strong fighter and a heavy puncher. But he had fought just once in the previous three years (a 10-round loss), having spent most of that time in prison. Ward had trained hard for Mamby and was in good shape. He also figured that the rust Mungin had accumulated while sitting in jail would be too much to overcome. Long layoffs have a way of taking their toll on a fighter's skills and, especially, his timing, and pushups and shadowboxing inside a prison cell are no substitute for the boxing gym.

Ward weighed 136 for the fight—four pounds below the junior welterweight limit—but Mungin showed up at the weigh-in a whopping 18 pounds heavier, at 154.

"Fuck this, we're going home!" bellowed Dicky, who understood what that kind of disadvantage could do to a fighter.[2] Their mom—Micky's manager—was on the same page. A furious argument ensued with Katz, who was trying to hold the promotion together, as Ward sat quietly by, trying to maintain his fighter's edge. Busloads of friends and fans were on their way from Lowell. Micky was trained and in shape. He was ready to fight, no matter who happened to be hulking in the opposing corner. Dicky stuck to his guns, but Micky also stuck to his. The show went on.

Mungin proved to be much too big, much too strong, and surprisingly sharp and skillful. Ward said later that fighting Mungin felt like pushing against a concrete wall. He couldn't move him and couldn't hurt him. His nose was bleeding, hindering his breathing, by the fourth round. In the sixth, Mungin snapped Ward's head back with an uppercut that scrambled his brain. According to Ward, it was the hardest punch he ever took. Seconds later, Mungin opened a gash over Ward's eye—a cut so bad that his legendary cutman, Eddie "The Clot" Aliano, struggled mightily to stem the bleeding.

In the sixth round, a hard right landed flush on the chin, putting Ward on his back. He got up and somehow managed to finish the fight on his feet, covered in his own blood. Mungin won a unanimous decision, and the knockdown proved to be the difference: Two of the three scorecards showed a one-point margin at the final bell.

The fact that Ward had been foolhardy enough to fight an opponent who was so much larger created a postfight incident in the dressing room: New Jersey trainer Carmen Graziano, whose clientele had included world champions Joey Giardello, Mike Rossman, Carl "The Truth" Williams, and Bruce Seldon, walked through the door, strutted right past Dicky, and shoved his card in Micky's hand.

"Give me a call if you ever want some help," Graziano told him, a clear slap at the other people in the room. "That was bullshit. You never should have fought that kid. You should have taken your money and gone home."[3]

Ward was now 17–2, but the Mungin loss did no damage to his reputation. He had been matched against a middleweight and had nearly won anyway, showing the kind of valor that brings television ratings. Promoter Bob Arum of Top Rank simply shrugged at the setback, realizing that Ward had been beaten by a surprisingly formidable fighter who was nowhere near the 140-pound weight class.

"They shouldn't have fought," Arum told the *Boston Globe*. "Losing in this case was no big deal."[4]

Arum then backed up the statement by announcing that Ward would be fighting for the NABF belt the following November, against a highly respected veteran, Harold Brazier, at the Boston Garden. What the promoter didn't know at the time was that Ward had reinjured his right hand in the loss to Mungin—a problem that was about to get worse with each subsequent day of training, swelling badly after each session on the heavy bag.

Fighting Brazier with a belt on the line was quickly determined to be a fool's errand—Micky and Dicky knew there was no way the hand would be useful again by November 15, the date set for the fight. But that didn't keep Ward from fighting. He was back in the ring three months after the Mungin loss, against Francisco Tomas da Cruz, a Brazilian who was 30–3, and knocked him out with a body shot in the third round. That led to an offer Ward decided he couldn't turn down—a shot at the USBA championship, against Frankie Warren, a 30-year-old who was both explosive and elusive.

Frankie "Panchito" Warren was a stump of a junior welterweight, standing just 5-foot-3—stature that made him an awkward and difficult opponent for a 5-foot-8 body-puncher like Ward. He was part of a tough boxing family from Corpus Christi, Texas (two brothers, Willie and Harold, also fought professionally), where he had compiled a stunning amateur record of 269 victories and just 11 losses. Warren won his first 23 fights as a pro, including a 10-round unanimous decision in 1986 over an undefeated James "Buddy" McGirt in Corpus Christi. That fight had been close enough to warrant a 1988 rematch for the IBF's vacant 140-pound crown, a sequel that McGirt dominated before scoring a 12th-round TKO to win the first of his three world titles.

Ward describes Warren as a "tiny, whirling beast of a fighter,"[5] saying he was experienced, skilled, and well schooled. He arrived with a solid game plan.

Warren's size and style were a puzzle from the opening bell, and by the time Ward began to find solutions, he was well behind on the scorecards. Warren won a unanimous decision, leaving Ward with a bruised ego and a pair of hands that were aching worse than ever.

By then, Ward also was living with his high school sweetheart, Laurie Ann Carroll. They had begun dating when he was 14 and she was 12, but the relationship was a stormy one and they had gone their separate ways when Micky was 17. The life of a fighter offers little in the way of stability, Ward explains. Dedication to boxing must take priority over life at home. Money comes in chunks—small ones, at least in the beginning—and vanishes quickly, which makes stress a constant companion. Boxers have no pension plan—usually, they have no long-term plan at all—which exacerbates that stress throughout the years. Pain and irritability are constant companions. It's not exactly the recipe to live happily ever after.

"He loved Laurie and could never get over her," his friend Tony Underwood told journalist Bob Halloran. "We had girls over all the time—two single guys—but he couldn't get another relationship started without having Laurie in the back of his mind."[6]

With two throbbing hands, Ward was fighting again on May 23, 1989—just four months after the loss to Warren. By then, Laurie was pregnant. Suddenly, Ward had more on his mind than boxing. He was having doubts about his boxing future, wondering whether he could convince the sport's power brokers, once again, that he was still a contender. It was a different kind of pressure than he'd ever experienced before.

He rose to the occasion in the ring, stopping Clarence Coleman, 13–3–1, in the fifth round to improve to 20–3. A month later, his daughter Kasie was born, an occasion he describes as the happiest day of his life. But by then, both of his damaged hands had become a huge problem. The pain after a fight was nearly intolerable. Beating on bags and sparring partners each day in the gym made healing an impossibility. Meanwhile, the buzz—Micky Ward is damaged goods, a shot fighter—was making its way back to him.

In February 1990, nine months after stopping Coleman, he fought David Rivello, 14–1, at Hynes Convention Center in Boston, and escaped with a split-decision victory. He had stepped into the ring that night for the first time as a pro without his longtime assistant trainer, Johnny Dunn, who had died of a heart attack just before Christmas.

Ward was once again a respected commodity in the junior welterweight division, with a record of 21–3 and a reputation for uncommon valor. Fighters like that tend to be rewarded—if not with riches, with gaudy trophy belts. Next up was another shot at a regional championship—the IBF's Intercontinental super lightweight title—against Harold Brazier. Brazier was 35 years old. He had 75 professional fights on his record. He was fearless and experienced, and he was anything but finished. Ward knew Brazier, despite his longevity, was still a fighter who could beat anyone on a given night.

By 1989—the year before Micky Ward fought Harold Brazier for the IBF Intercontinental junior welterweight belt—his trainer and half-brother, Dicky Eklund, was so strung out on cocaine that he became one of the "stars" of the HBO documentary *High on Crack Street: The Lost Lives of Lowell*, which, perhaps ironically, was coproduced by a distant cousin, Richie Farrell (Dicky's maternal grandmother and Richie's paternal grandmother were sisters).

The film made its debut six years later, in 1995, and won multiple awards, but Dicky regards it with enormous disdain and claims his cousin—a recovering heroin addict himself—and other members of the film crew quite literally financed some of the crack cocaine he used to get high for the cameras.

"They fed me crack cocaine, and they paid for a lot of it. Even the kid that did the documentary, my distant cousin Richie Farrell, has said that he wouldn't do it again if he had the chance," Dicky said. "I'm not afraid to share my story, but when you're feeding somebody crack at their lowest point, of course they're going to do something like that."[7]

The documentary is simultaneously riveting and bleak, as it tells the story of Lowell's decomposition from a vibrant textile city of the 1920s to the boarded-up, broken-down shell of a town it had become by the 1980s.

The signature scene of *High on Crack Street* might be the moment when Dicky—gaunt, skinny, and colorless—sits in a dilapidated crack house among other addicts and looks directly into the camera, and, with his brain swimming in the drug, puts the irony of his sad situation into the sharpest-possible focus: "I fought Sugar Ray Leonard on HBO," he says.[8]

That moment erased any ambiguity about whether Dicky understood what he had done to himself and what he was still doing. Even as the cocaine warmed his veins and induced its irresistible euphoria, he remained rational enough to grasp that he had squandered what might have been a championship-level boxing career, blown any shot at financial comfort, blackened the family name, done irreparable damage to his closest relationships, and gone from town hero to local thug and criminal—and, at that moment, he regarded all of those things as collateral damage. Like every addict, he was willing to sacrifice every bit of it for his next hit.

"I used crack cocaine once, and the rest of the time it used me. I was addicted instantly," Dicky says. "I really even hate to describe the effect crack has on your body, because the feeling, that first time, is so good that you know it's eventually going to kill you, because you won't be able to resist doing it again and again."

If his producer/cousin wasn't (allegedly) handing him cash to buy the drug, Dicky was committing strong-arm robberies on street corners or masquerading as an undercover cop, shaking down others who had wandered into Lowell's meanest neighborhoods looking for a prostitute or a fix of their own. He occasionally teamed up with a local streetwalker to lure his victims. She would lead their mark into a dark hallway or alley and confirm that he was carrying a wallet full of money, and Dicky would show up and take it away. During his multiday binges, Dicky, the trainer, usually was nowhere to be found, leaving his brother to train alone. And then, inexplicably, he'd wander back into the gym, outrun the fighter during roadwork, and give Micky all he wanted in sparring, as if he'd been there all along.

For his part, Micky smoldered, sometimes boiling over, but he had become acutely aware that there was no drill powerful enough to penetrate his big brother's granite skull. Dicky had become as adept at deflecting another person's anger as he once had been at evading an opponent's punches. And for all their flaws, fights, and dysfunction, the Wards were bound by unconditional family love. The matriarch, Alice, chose to pretend all was well with her firstborn son, undoubtedly because accepting the reality was too painful. And Micky realized that his own boxing career represented Dicky's best chance at turning his life around. All the while, Micky clearly understood that his chances of becoming a world champion and fulfilling his own dreams would have been greatly enhanced by replacing his ne'er-do-well sibling with a reputable trainer—someone he could actually count on. But blood was thicker than water.

With a few beers in his system, Micky went looking for his big brother one night after not seeing him at the gym in a couple of days. He found him in a crack house on Branch Street, a place Dicky was known to hang out, bursting through the door and confronting the junkies he found there. When they denied seeing Dicky, Ward stormed from room to room, frightening and intimidating anyone in his path, finally finding his brother cowering behind a shower curtain. After making a brief, angry attempt at an intervention, Ward pivoted and walked away, realizing his brother wasn't in any condition to listen to reason. He didn't even listen when he was sober.

The night before his fight with Harold Brazier, Ward went to bed early in his Atlantic City hotel room. In the adjoining room, Dicky hosted a loud, all-night party. The next night, a sleepless and listless Ward lost 10 out of 12 rounds to Brazier.

That defeat was the first of a four-fight skid. Six months later, he dropped another lopsided 12-round decision to undefeated Charles Murray. The next year, 1991, he lost back-to-back 10-round decisions to Tony Martin and Ricky Meyers. Brazier, Murray, Martin, and Meyers had a combined win–loss record of 121–14–1—there was no real shame in losing to any of them—but four straight defeats represent a death spiral for any fighter's career. And there was also a physical price to pay. At this point of his career, Ward already had suffered multiple concussions, and both of his hands were in perpetual agony. It is the type of toll every warrior endures as his career wears on: Injuries and reinjuries stop healing the way they did when the fighter was young, thereby accelerating the aging process. Ward, only in his mid-20s, was already wondering if retirement was near.

Ward identifies the loss to Meyers as a low point. He had become a tired, broken-down fighter. His relationship with his girlfriend Laurie— the mother of his child—was in similar ruins. The television networks and promoters had written him off. And—maybe the worst part of all for a fighter—his hunger was gone.

All of that came crashing down on him as he sat with Dicky in the dressing room of Harrah's Trump Plaza Hotel after the loss to Meyers. "Fuck it," he remembers saying to Dicky, according to Bob Halloran's Ward bio *Irish Thunder*. "I'm not going to be a punching bag anymore. Let them find someone else to pad their record. I'm done."

Imagine the feeling, waking up in the morning to confront the reality that the part of your life you have treasured the most is over—at age 26.

Micky Ward had been a boxing star in Lowell, Massachusetts, since his preteen years. He had fought multiple times on ESPN. He had packed arenas, walking from his dressing room to the ring in a searing spotlight, with thousands of people cheering, chanting his name, shouting encouragement. He had signed autographs and posed for photos with people he'd never met and would never see again. He'd been held as a role model to children. He had been chased by beautiful women.

And then, it was over. When a one-time contender loses two, three, or, in Ward's case, four in a row, there are two possible paths: soldier on as cannon fodder for hot, young prospects who apparently have a future or hang up the gloves, save what's left of your beat-up brain and body, and fade anonymously into the rat race with everyone else.

He was on a four-fight skid—albeit against strong opponents—and his phone no longer was ringing. Any cache he once had among promoters and matchmakers had evaporated into a fog of mediocrity. Fighters turn professional with dreams of someday cashing in on their hard work. Promoters enter the sport with the same idea—cashing in on the boxer's hard work. If that boxer no longer has audience appeal, he might as well be a dirty Kleenex.

Ward had undoubtedly been a victim of a series of bad decisions by his mother/manager and by Top Rank promoter Bob Arum, whose matchmaking motives weren't always in a fighter's best interest, but he blamed no one but himself for the flameout. No one had forced him to sign any of his fight contracts. No one had pushed him into the ring. And he wasn't naïve about the nature of the game: Win and you're golden. Lose and you're yesterday's news. Plus, Ward had been going 10 rounds per fight against a steady parade of formidable opponents—men trained to bring the pain—and despite the valor he showed in the ring night after night, he suffered from attrition.

By the time he lost to Ricky Meyers, Ward understood that he wasn't the same fighter he'd been a couple of years earlier. He wasn't focused, and he no longer was hungry. So, he walked away, the way a man might walk away from a faded romance. The embers had burned out.

In the winter of 1992, he took a job as a correctional officer—a guard—at the Middlesex County House of Corrections in Billerica, Massachusetts, a facility where his brother Dicky had spent more than a few nights as an inmate. In fact, a good sampling of the occupants were men he'd known in school or on the streets, and an even larger part of the population knew the celebrity boxer named Micky Ward.

It's a mind trip to be "washed up" at age 26—to go from a celebrity who rarely has to pay for his own beer to just another hamster on the wheel. Ward suffered from boredom and claustrophobia at the jail, and Laurie had left him. She'd had enough of the dark, surly attitude that had enveloped him since his retirement. He was drinking too much. He was delving into cocaine—despite his acute understanding of the toll it had taken on so many others, including Dicky. And he was coming home every night to an empty house. He found his job to be boring, undemanding, and suffocating.

Most of all, he was suddenly without a method to release any pent-up energy and anxiety.

In the summer of 1993, Ward began to purge that energy at a small gym in Tewksbury, Massachusetts, pounding the heavy bag and the speed bag, skipping rope, and sparring. He was two years removed from boxing, and not yet 29 years old, when he began to feel the hunger pangs again. His hands were suddenly pain-free for the first time since his teens. His mind felt clear and focused. He began to crave more time in the gym—time that his regimented shifts at the jail couldn't accommodate. So, he turned in his resignation and went back to highway construction, where the pay was decent and the hours were more flexible.

Whether or not he fully realized it at the time, Ward was angling toward a return to the sport. His body felt rejuvenated. His strength and timing were back. He was excited again. But life has a way of interfering with dreams at inopportune times.

In November 1993, Ward was driving a five-ton back roller with a crew that was repaving the parking lot of a Costco store. His job required him to leap off the roller several times a day and use a metal tamper to smooth out sections of the pavement that could not be flattened by the machine. His method, he said, was to stop the roller, toss the tamper over the side, and jump six feet to the ground to finish grooming the area. What happened that day—three days before Thanksgiving—is the type of thing a novelist might dream up as the fate of a villain who loses a fight with James Bond.

Ward stopped his roller next to a concrete island in the parking lot and set the brake. He dropped the tamper to the pavement and leaped off after it. The tamper didn't land flat on the ground, as it had thousands of times before. Instead, it lodged upright, it's long handle pointing toward the sky like a spear. Ward dropped six feet from the driver's seat to the ground, landing directly on the now-vertical rod.

"The tamper hit me square in the ass, like a dart burrowing into a bull's-eye," Ward relates. "The tip of the handle pierced my denim jeans, shredded my thermal underwear, and funneled its way parallel to my anus and rectum, literally ripping me a new asshole in the process."[9]

Doctors later told him that if the strike had been an inch closer to the center, the handle would have impaled his stomach or esophagus, probably killing him instantly. Instead, it cut a four-inch swath alongside his rectum. He stood impaled, unable to move, unable to even fall down, until his coworkers finally heard him wailing for help and discovered the gruesome scene. He was rushed by ambulance to the University of Massachusetts Memorial Medical Center in Worcester, where doctors performed reconstructive surgery, discovering in the process that the muscles holding Ward's sphincter in place had been ripped apart. His bowels needed to be reassembled.

Ward said the four days he spent in the hospital were the worst of his life. He was wracked with pain unlike anything he had ever experienced or imagined. His recovery took four months, during which time he gobbled Vicodin and slept 12 to 15 hours a day. He was completely dependent on visiting home nurses for routine things like going to the bathroom and eating his meals. He was unable to hold his young daughter in his arms. But he was grateful that he was still alive and focused on getting a bit healthier every day. Anything else in his life would have to wait.

For Micky Ward, 1993 had seemed like a lifetime. In addition to the freak accident that had nearly killed him at the construction site, his brother Dicky was arrested three times that year for crimes that were escalating in nature. On one of those occasions, Alice Ward let her son stew behind bars for four months before finally bailing him out. She had paid his bail too many times before.

In fact, Bob Halloran writes about a 1987 incarceration during which Dicky's mother organized a $5-a-head fundraiser at the local VFW to try to raise the $5,000 she needed to get him out of jail on that occasion. The centerpiece of the event was a showing of Dicky's fight with Sugar Ray Leonard. When only about 30 people showed up, Micky dipped into his own pocket for the money.

Six years later, the situation was far direr. After 27 arrests, Dicky was facing life in prison as a habitual offender for a laundry list of charges of carjacking, kidnapping, armed robbery with a sawed-off shotgun, unlawful possession of ammunition, carrying an unlicensed firearm, breaking and entering with intent to commit a felony, larceny under $250, and possession of burglary tools. He also didn't endear himself to the judge when he showed up drunk and late for his court date, which had to be rescheduled. He eventually accepted a generous plea bargain, declaring himself guilty of the charges and accepting eight years in prison. He served a little more than half of the term, during which Alice raised his sons, Dickie Jr. and Tommy, and his daughter, Kerry.

"Good-bye, Dicky," she said. "Maybe this is for the best. You'll come out stronger and healthier. I know you will, honey. You're a good boy."[10]

In a 2011 interview with the authors of this book, Dicky said that four-year period saved his life. "It was absolutely the best thing that ever happened," he said. "I was going to be dead on the streets. I probably would have gotten killed, eventually, but I was very close to dying when I was sent to jail. I was down to 118 pounds when I went in. I actually saw myself in a mirror at one point and I starting crying, thinking, 'I don't know who this guy is.'"[11]

The sight of his emaciated, drug-ravaged body was only part of the wake-up call, Dicky said. He also came to realize, at long last, what others had been trying to drum into his head for years. "I woke up in jail every day and realized I was separated from my kids, I was separated from my family, and I was no good to nobody," he said. "When I was on the streets, I always said to my mother and everybody, 'I'm not hurting nobody but myself. What's the big deal?' When I went to prison, I started to wake up. I started praying to God. And I finally realized I had affected a lot of lives."[12]

One of those who was affected—his brother Micky—was more angry than sympathetic, not only toward Dicky, but also toward his father, George Ward, who, in 1993, also was on his way to prison. He had been convicted of bilking an 80-year-old woman with Alzheimer's disease out of her life savings through his roofing business, collecting $90,000 from her without doing any work. In a separate case, an 89-year-old woman claimed he defrauded her of more than $20,000 the same way. So, at age 54, George Ward was sentenced to two to four years in Middlesex County Jail.

Micky did the only logical thing: He moved on with his own life.

When his injuries had adequately healed, he went back to work with the paving crew during the day and drank most nights with other neighborhood guys at the Highland Tap. Then, one day, he crossed paths with an old friend, Mickey O'Keefe, the Lowell police officer who had helped train Dicky and him, on and off, since their amateur days. O'Keefe offered him a bit of advice that Ward was dying to hear.

"You've got a lot left in the tank, Mick," he said, according to Halloran's book *Irish Thunder*. "Don't waste it."

Ward didn't really have to be convinced. He was already on that page. He knew by then that he wanted to give boxing another chance while he was still young enough to make it happen. He didn't want to look back on his life with regret and wonder what might have been.

O'Keefe, once a hard drinker himself, recognized that Ward had been imbibing too much and coaxed him into Alcoholics Anonymous, where he ultimately embraced the fact that he'd had a problem with booze for years. The meetings at AA introduced Ward to people whose lives had been devastated by substance abuse—people he didn't want to become. He returned to the West End Gym sober, determined, with renewed vigor, and with O'Keefe in his corner day after day. Later, O'Keefe opened his own gym, called Lowell Boxing, in the "Acre," where Ward's boxing renovation moved to a new level.

In June 1994, seven months after the construction accident, Micky Ward returned to the ring in the ballroom of the Lowell Sheraton to fight Luis Castillo in a 10-rounder for $400—a bit of a pay cut from the $17,000 he had earned against Mike Mungin. Only a few hundred people showed up to watch.

For Ward, it was a humbling comedown from his not-too-distant past, when he was fighting on the Leonard–Hagler card in Las Vegas or packing the house as the headliner at some Atlantic City casino. But, in fact, he was happy to be fighting for peanuts for a small gaggle of people. After recovering from the traumatic accident in the Costco parking lot, Ward merely wanted to quietly gather evidence that would tell him whether he still had the goods.

Micky took his time against Castillo, who had a 5–10 record and had won just once in his previous eight fights. In the fifth round, Ward delivered a left hook to the body that folded his opponent in half and ended the fight. It was the first small step in a careful, calculated comeback, which, during the next 21 months, saw Ward remove the rust, a little at a time, against the likes of Genaro Andujar (8–10–1), Edgardo Rosario (pro debut), Alberto Alicea (6–31) and Alex Ortiz (0–5)—four fights, all knockouts, totaling eight rounds.

In April 1996, in front of 6,000 rowdy spectators at the Fleet Center in Boston, Ward took on Louis "The Viper" Veader, 31–0, the first significant opponent of his comeback. Veader, from Providence, Rhode Island, had a record fattened against opponents with losing records and minimal credentials, the only marquee name on his resume being that of former WBA lightweight champion Livingstone Bramble, whom he'd fought a year and a half earlier. By then, Bramble was long past his salad days, with a record of 37–13–3.

For the 26-year-old Veader, who had knocked out 13 of his 31 opponents, Ward represented the first real test of his six-year pro career, the first true threat to his unblemished record. An "international" junior welterweight title belt offered by the World Boxing Union—a sanctioning body with virtually no recognition value—would be on the line.

The 30-year-old Ward, 28–7, with 18 knockouts, showed up in the best shape of his career and controlled the first two rounds, opening a cut over Veader's eye. Then, an odd and frightening thing happened. Veader planted a hard shot into Ward's chest that made him swoon, nearly knocking him out. Suddenly, he felt his heart pounding quickly—pumping with frightening velocity. He suspected he might be having a heart attack.

Then, weirder still, he felt his heartbeat slow down, seemingly hesitating between beats. He also couldn't breathe. Ward was in a full-blown panic, wondering if he might die in the ring, but—typical of a boxer—rather than quitting, he persevered, slowing his pace, hoping the problem would correct itself. By the sixth round, his pulse felt normal again, his fear diminished, and he began to rally.

In the eighth round, he ripped Veader with a hard left hook, putting him on the canvas. Midway through the ninth, Ward caught him with a body shot against the ropes and watched him double over in agony. That one ended the fight. It was Ward's sixth-straight knockout victory.

After the fight, Ward looked into ESPN's TV cameras and spoke to his still-incarcerated relatives. "I just want to say hello to my brother, Dicky. This is for you, Dick. I love you," he said. "And for my father: I love you."

Then he headed back to Lowell and went straight to a victory party at the Tap Room, where, once again, he was the central attraction. For his hometown fans, Micky Ward was back.

He had possibilities in his life again, including a potential six-digit payday against the winner of an upcoming megafight between two of the biggest stars in the history of the sport, Oscar De La Hoya and Julio Cesar Chavez. Another possibility was Gabriel Ruelas, the former WBC super featherweight titlist.

Postfight tests revealed that Ward had suffered from a heart murmur during the Veader fight, a problem he'd probably been born with. Doctors gave him a green light to continue his career, but neither Ruelas nor the De La Hoya–Chavez winner seemed likely, after closer scrutiny. Ruelas, a natural 135-pounder, would have to move up in weight to face Ward, and De La Hoya and Chavez figured to have glitzier opportunities on the table than a fight with Ward, who, after all, had seven losses on his record.

Three months after the first Veader fight, Ward beat him again, this time in a tough, 12-round decision. For Veader, the second loss to Ward essentially marked the end of his career. He would fight just once more—a victory over an insignificant opponent—before retiring for good.

In an interview for this book, Veader said he stopped because he got frustrated, having earned $20,000, combined, for the two Micky Ward fights—the biggest paychecks of his career.

"I had a daughter from a previous relationship, so I just had to start working. I made money working, so I decided to go back to driving a truck, like I'd always done," he said.

Ward came away from the second Veader fight with another second-tier bauble for his trophy case, the WBC Intercontinental title belt.

Meanwhile, things were eroding behind the scenes in Ward's camp, although symptoms wouldn't evolve into full-blown problems for a while. Sal LoNano, a friend of Ward's father, had first walked into Mickey O'Keefe's gym to watch Micky's workouts before the first Veader fight. O'Keefe, the street-smart cop, was immediately suspicious of Lo-Nano, who had a reputation in some circles as a blowhard and a wannabe wise guy. On the day before the first Veader bout, O'Keefe confronted the man he saw as a potential vulture, according to *Irish Thunder*. "What the hell are you coming around here for?" he growled at LoNano.

"I'm just making sure Micky's okay."

"Well, who the fuck are you?"

"I'm a friend of his father. He asked me to keep an eye on Micky."

Micky remembered LoNano as a person who had watched many of his early fights and considered him an okay guy. He also saw him as a successful businessman—LoNano owned an automotive business and cab company in South Boston. With a nudge from his father, Ward invited LoNano to become involved as his manager.

LoNano, who had no experience in boxing, hit the ground running, making a deal no one was really expecting. Five weeks after the second Veader bout, on Labor Day 1996, LoNano negotiated a Las Vegas fight between Micky and the man who was considered one of the best pound-for-pound fighters of all time, Julio Cesar Chavez. Ward's payday—$100,000—would be the largest of his career. Suddenly, the new manager had credibility with Micky Ward.

Chavez, who was 96–2–1, remained a god in the sport, even though he'd been stopped in four rounds by De La Hoya in June 1996. In September, he had rebounded by stopping highly respected Joey Gamache (45–2). Team Chavez clearly viewed Micky Ward as a relatively safe pawn in a larger game. "El Gran Campion Mexico" could obliterate this respected tough guy, then move back into the sweepstakes for the A-list opponents of the 140-pound weight class. Chavez also was deeply indebted to the Mexican government for back taxes and needed what he saw as an easy payday.

It was a much different perspective for Team Ward. Upsetting Chavez would open any number of doors.

With such high stakes, LoNano arranged for everyone to get away from potential distractions in Lowell and train for six weeks at 10,000 feet above sea level in the isolated mountain town of Big Bear Lake, California. He also brought in a second trainer, Jimmy Connolly, and almost immediately elevated him over O'Keefe. To put it mildly, that didn't sit well with the man who had helped nurture Micky since his youth and, more importantly, been the one and only architect of his comeback to this point.

It's an age-old story in boxing. One trainer is mother hen to a fighter, often from boyhood to the early days of his pro career. Then, when the stakes get higher and the money gets bigger, a more experienced manager enters the scene, and his first move is to bolster the brainpower in the gym and the corner by importing another trainer. Sometimes it works, sometimes it doesn't. What never changes is that someone's ego becomes irreparably bruised.

When Connolly explained that new orders had been passed down from LoNano, O'Keefe ricocheted off the ceiling. "Fuck that!" he yelled. "I know Micky better than any of you. I've been working with him every day. When nobody else is there, it's Micky and me."[13]

The chemistry of the new Team Ward soon was put to the acid test. Five days before the bout, Julio Cesar Chavez pulled out, claiming a hand injury. The scuttlebutt was that Chavez might have hurt his hand not during training camp, but after punching his brother-in-law, and that he also had distracting personal problems stemming from a volatile custody dispute with his wife. Whatever the case, Bob Arum wanted $20,000 in expense money back from Team Ward. Most of it was already spent.

O'Keefe wanted to know why they should have to pay it back. It wasn't their fault the fight had been cancelled. LoNano apparently had already made that argument and lost. Arum had another opponent lined up: Manny Castillo, a club fighter with a 13–6–2 record.

O'Keefe hit the roof, not wanting to accept a fight against a substitute opponent they knew virtually nothing about, and became angrier when he was overruled. Then, the situation got worse. Only hours before the opening bell in Reno, LoNano came into the dressing room with more bad news: Arum had told him Ward's purse wouldn't be the $100,000 he'd been promised for fighting Chavez, but just $10,000, since the opponent was Castillo.

O'Keefe blew a gasket and insisted they walk out. LoNano, who suddenly had big financial problems, resisted. Ward ultimately made the same kind of decision he'd made so many other times in his career. "I'll fight him," he said. Bottom line: $10,000 was $10,000.

Things immediately went from bad to worse. In the first round, Ward threw a body punch and ripped a tendon off the bone of his right thumb. He fought nine more rounds—the first several in excruciating pain, then with numbness in the right hand—and escaped with a split decision over the no-name opponent from Mexico.

After the return flight from Reno to Boston's Logan Airport, O'Keefe, still seething, refused to accept a ride home from LoNano. He also made it clear that he held Ward responsible for creating the rift by allowing outsiders into their previously exclusive relationship. The damage, on multiple levels, would last for years.

In April 1997, four months after the Reno debacle, Ward was back in Nevada, fighting on HBO at the Thomas & Mack Center in Las Vegas with a surgically repaired left thumb, but without his lifelong friend, Mickey O'Keefe, who was still boiling about being demoted by LoNano to assistant trainer.

Once again, Jimmy Connolly was the lead man in the corner as Ward took on Alfonso "Poncho" Sanchez, who brought a 16–0 record—and 15 KOs—with him from Tijuana. Because Sanchez had a reputation as a big puncher, Team Ward's game plan was to stick and move, staying out of harm's way as much as possible, and outpoint the 25-year-old Mexican.

Ward said later he felt sluggish that night, for unknown reasons. He was knocked down in the fifth round and was well behind on the scorecards late in the fight, fighting so poorly that Connolly threatened to throw in the towel. Meanwhile, Ward also was being drubbed by the HBO broadcast tandem, Jim Lampley and Larry Merchant, who opined that he no longer belonged in a professional ring and should retire for his own good.

But in the seventh round, Ward bent Sanchez's ribcage with a body shot and landed a two-punch combination—the first to the head, the next to the ribs. Suddenly, a bored crowd—fans who were anxiously awaiting the headliner between Oscar De La Hoya and Pernell Whitaker—came to life. Castillo crumbled to the canvas, crawled a few feet on his hands and knees, and rolled onto his side and took the 10-count.

It wasn't quite a rags-to-riches moment. It was more like coming off life support and discovering you can breathe on your own again. After pulling the Castillo fight out of the fire, Ward was offered a chance to fight Vince Phillips (36–3) for the IBF super lightweight title at the Roxy in Boston. This is where the dream would become a reality, at long last. Micky Ward was finally going to get a world title shot. But not every dream is a pleasant one.

Phillips was a skilled boxer and heavy-handed puncher from Pensacola, Florida, who had won the crown three months earlier from previously undefeated Kostya Tszyu, a future International Boxing Hall of Famer, and the fact that he was willing to fight on Ward's home turf spoke volumes about his confidence. He had two losses on his record—one at the hands of Anthony Jones in 1993, the other versus WBA champ Ike Quartey, 31–0, 16 months before the Ward fight.

Ward was 30–7—9–0 since his comeback—and a solid underdog against Phillips, but he couldn't have cared less about what the bookmakers thought. To get a world title fight in his hometown felt like a dream come true. But dreams are capricious. They can change in an instant.

A minute into the third round, Ward felt a trickle of blood in his left eye and knew he had a problem. The trickle became a waterfall. Referee Dick Flaherty immediately stopped the action and summoned the ring doctor, Patricia Joffi, who inspected the wound with a flashlight.

"I'm sorry, Micky. I can see right to the bone."

"Fuck no! Let me fight," Ward raged. "Give us a chance to work on it!"

"I'm sorry," she said. [14]

And that was that. The fight was over, and Ward's first world title opportunity was gone. The crowd (including Ward's sisters and their husbands and boyfriends) rained cups of beer and other projectiles into the ring. Phillips was berated with racial epithets, the same type of invective Sugar Ray Leonard had experienced the night he'd beaten Dicky Eklund in Lowell.

Already angry, Micky leaned over the ropes in a rage. "Stop it!" he screamed at his family. "It's not his fault!"

Ward's initial frustration with Dr. Joffi subsided a bit later that night when a second doctor checked the injury in the hospital emergency room. The injury was so severe, the doctor told Ward, that one more punch could have cost him his sight in that eye. Ward subsequently expressed remorse that Joffi had incurred such wrath, not only from the crowd, but also from Ward, himself, after stopping the fight. He apologized and thanked her the next time they met.

"Live to fight another day" is a hard philosophy for a boxer to embrace, but Micky Ward moved on.

# 7

# CROSSROADS

If a football, basketball, or baseball team struggles through a bad year, it is, by design, a temporary problem. The season ends, the off-season comes and goes, and the team starts fresh with an undefeated record—0–0—on opening day the following year.

Not so with boxing. An unbeaten fighter carries an aura of invincibility. He's never been conquered, which brings with it the possibility—usually irrational and grandiose—that he cannot be conquered. With his first loss, the boxer loses that magic cloak forever. Any opponent, from that day onward, can take solace in the knowledge that the man in the opposite corner is vulnerable in some way. Someone already has proven that.

There are no seasons in boxing. A loss blemishes a fighter's record until the end of time as evidence of his vulnerability. He'll never be undefeated again. Each subsequent defeat drags him a bit closer to the "ordinary" label, depending on the quality of the opponent who conquered him. Countless fighters call it a career after their second or third loss.

The loss to Vince Phillips in August 1997 was the eighth of Micky Ward's 38-fight career, firmly entrenching him among the sport's class of also-rans. Fighters who are 30–8 don't get world title shots with six- or seven-digit paydays. If they appear on television, it is on the coattails of someone younger and hotter. He's not the one the public is paying to see.

Ward understood that his blown opportunity against Phillips would almost certainly represent his last chance at a world title belt. But he remained motivated by the fact that the loss to Phillips had been due, at least in part, to "extenuating circumstances." Ward wasn't beaten down by Phillips—unforgivable to boxing promoters, matchmakers, and fans. He was stopped by a nasty cut that impaired his vision, which usually falls into the "tough luck" category. Tough-luck fighters sometimes float back to the surface and get another shot. Those fighters also feel—often rightfully—that things could have (even would have) been different if their luck had been better. So, in such cases, it's not unusual to see them fight on.

"Relax," Sal LoNano told Ward after the Phillips fight. "No one's disappointed in you."[1]

Indeed, promoter Bob Arum and Top Rank, his high-powered promotional company, chalked up the loss to misfortune.

Ward was back in the ring eight months later against a fighter of minimal skill and virtually no threat, Mark Fernandez, who brought a record of 33–17–1 to Foxwoods Resort in April 1998. Fernandez collapsed from a body shot in the third round and didn't get up. That cleared the path for Ward to challenge an up-and-coming star, 20-year-old Zab Judah, who was 15–0, with blinding speed and mad boxing skills—a fighter already being compared to the best 140-pounders in the world.

It was another big opportunity for Ward to demonstrate that he wasn't washed up, that he could still be entrusted to bang with the best. But he would be moving forward, once again, without his friend and longtime trainer Mickey O'Keefe, who had stormed out of Ward's training camp just before the Fernandez fight after LoNano once again brought in a second trainer, Rupert "Nell" Brown.

LoNano's edict was that O'Keefe would remain in charge of day-to-day training and conditioning, but Brown would be the man in Ward's corner, giving the fighter instructions and strategy between rounds on fight night. O'Keefe's reaction left no room for interpretation. F-bombs were exchanged. He challenged LoNano to a fight. Ward intervened, trying to calm the situation, to no avail. From where O'Keefe stood, the fighter was more to blame than the others for disrupting a once-harmonious (at least, in O'Keefe's mind) situation. They never worked together again, and Ward says they barely spoke until well after he retired.

The fight with Judah took place June 7, 1998, at Miccosukee Indian Gaming Resort in Miami, with an unimportant regional title belt on the line from the USBA. Ward took the young star 12 rounds but lost nearly every round and was hit with three times as many punches as he landed.

He later applauded Judah as "probably the best all-around fighter I ever faced." Judah later lived up to Ward's praise, winning five world championships in his career.

At age 33, having lost two of his last three fights, Micky Ward's boxing career had reached the " What's the point?" stage. He was banged up and rudderless, the kind of fallback opponent that a promoter might call as an afterthought, after all of the more interesting options had been exhausted, or when a first choice had been injured.

A ray of sunlight in Ward's otherwise drab boxing picture broke through the clouds when his brother Dicky was released from prison after more than 3 1/2 years, his system scrubbed clean of drugs and alcohol by the state of Massachusetts. He rejoined society with a new outlook to go along with his pristine blood tests.

"I decided I was going to make something out of my life and help others avoid the mistakes I'd made," Dicky said in a 2011 interview on the *Ringside Boxing Show*. "The judge did me a favor: Those words, '10 to 15,' helped turn my life around."[2]

Once he got out, Ward assumed the big-brother role for Dicky and felt okay with it. He still loved his older sibling, and, perhaps more than ever, they needed one another. Dicky emerged from prison with the new attitude his family had been hoping to see for years. He began sharing his story with at-risk kids on the streets and in boxing gyms, describing how he'd gone from a hero's life—a guy who once fought Sugar Ray Leonard on HBO—to that of a drunk and drug-addled gutter punk who robbed and roughed up ordinary citizens in pursuit of his next fix.

As expected, he also resumed his duties as Micky's primary trainer, this time with a brotherly dedication he hadn't shown in years. But Micky was on the shelf for the first seven months of his brother's freedom, recovering from complicated hand surgery that included removing damaged cartilage, scraping the bones, then rebuilding with bone from Ward's pelvis.

Those problems had started with the incident at the Cosmo, he was certain. They were injuries that might have healed properly, with no ill effects, for a normal person. But a boxer with hand injuries isn't normal. With nothing to lose and a lot to gain, Ward looked forward to the surgery. The procedure was a success. Micky returned to the ring on March 17, 1999—St. Patrick's Day—against Jose Luis Mendez, who dropped to 3–12–1 after Ward knocked him out in three rounds.

But a second surgery became necessary after the Mendez fight, when Ward's hand began hurting again. His doctor remedied the problem by removing one of the three screws he had installed during the first operation, which was irritating a bone. The bone transplant healed in a month, and Micky's manager, Sal LoNano, teamed with Al Valenti and ESPN's East Coast boxing coordinator, Russell Peltz, to put together a show at New Hampshire's Hampton Beach Casino that included Ward and a 25-year-old fighter with a 17–2 record named Jermal Corbin. LoNano took out a second mortgage and borrowed money from his mother-in-law—$125,000 in all—to finance the event on July 16, 1999.

Ward and Corbin were part of the undercard, but they were bumped to the featured fight when the main event between Bryant Brannon and Demetrius Davis fell apart at the last minute. Dicky, ever the street hustler, saw an opening for his brother. He told Peltz and the promoters that his brother wouldn't come out for the main event without more money. They ponied up another $2,500.

Ward's body attack broke down Corbin in five rounds. LoNano's roll of the dice wound up costing him about $1,000, which, considering the risk he took, was deemed a success.

Micky Ward already had defied the odds multiple times, rising from the ashes to extend a career that, by all rights, should have been over years earlier, but he was experienced and intuitive enough to realize that his fight with Reggie Green in October 1999 represented the end of the road if he didn't win.

The fight at the Icenter in Salem, New Hampshire, was scheduled three days before his 34th birthday. Ward already had lost nine times in his career, including two of his last four. If he couldn't beat Green, he saw no point in putting his already-battered body through any additional trauma. Desperation is what makes the sport appealing, and whatever allure the matchmaker saw stemmed from that.

Green, at this point, also felt like a cornered animal. The Clinton, Maryland, resident was just six months removed from the biggest fight—and also the biggest disappointment—of his seven-year professional career. In April, he'd been given his first world title opportunity, a shot at the WBA's 140-pound strap held by Sharmba Mitchell, and had come tantalizingly close, losing by majority decision. One judge scored the fight even, while the other two gave Mitchell, the defending champ, a narrow edge.

The 31-year-old Green understood that he, too, was potentially staring down the barrel of oblivion if he lost to Ward, who, by now, was clearly entrenched in that unfortunate boxing brotherhood known as "opponent"—a guy a matchmaker brought in as a respectable-but-safe challenge for a fighter who is trying to find his way back to the fast lane. Losing a second-straight fight—this one to a long-in-the-tooth, 33–9 fighter—was probably tantamount to a bus ticket to Palookaville.

Whatever played out would be seen by an ESPN television audience—Ward's 24th appearance on the network.

"If I can't beat a guy like Micky Ward, who's a tough, seasoned, veteran, I shouldn't even deserve to be fighting for world championships," Green told ESPN's cameras in advance of the fight.

With seconds remaining in the third round, Green, 30–3, sent Ward stumbling into the ropes—the bottom and second rope kept him standing—with a shot that turned his lip into hamburger. Ward later said it might have been the hardest punch he ever felt and speculated that if it had landed on his chin, rather than square in the mouth, he would have been knocked out. As it was, he managed to survive the round and make it back to his corner, where one of the magical cutmen, Al Gavin, went to work on the tattered remains of his lip.

Gavin had done his apprenticeship at Brooklyn's famed Stillman's Gym, the training headquarters of almost any world champion or top-drawer challenger who was preparing for a fight at Madison Square Garden. Its alumni, too plentiful to list in full, included such fighters as Jack Dempsey, Sugar Ray Robinson, Gene Tunney, Rocky Marciano, Jersey Joe Walcott, Joe Louis, Willie Pep, and Sandy Saddler. His tutors included a Who's Who of legendary boxing cornermen, including Ray Arcel, Whitey Bimstein, Chickie Ferrara, and Freddie Brown.

"It was a massive cut—big enough for Al to insert two fingers at once," Ward writes in *A Warrior's Heart*. "It was the kind of cut that, when it occurs anywhere else on the face, is enough to stop a fight. And if it had gotten any worse, it might have stopped this one."

Ward also remembered that Dicky lifted him off his stool at the bell to start the fourth round and had to support him momentarily to keep him from toppling over in the corner. Ward bounced on his toes before moving toward Green in the center of the ring, but his legs remained wobbly in the opening seconds of round four.

Fortunately for Ward, his opponent didn't go for the kill. He fought conservatively, perhaps recovering the energy he'd spent in the closing seconds of the previous round, and allowed Ward to recover some stability in his legs. Indeed, he landed 14 power shots on Green in the next three minutes to get back into the fight. Gavin was given another challenge when Green split Ward's cheekbone in the seventh round.

"Ward's face is a mess," declared Bob Papa, ESPN's ringside blow-by-blow announcer, with 30 seconds left in the round. "But the problem for Ward might be the problem in the mouth—all the blood he's been swallowing since round 3."

By the 10th round, the task facing Ward was clear. A fight that had seemed fairly even through six rounds had swung his opponent's way. In rounds 7 through 9, Green had landed 20 or more punches in each round. Ward had landed 26, total, in all three rounds. He knew he needed a knockout to win. Bloody and exhausted, he dug deep to attack Green from the bell, finally catching him with a left hand that sent him reeling into the ropes with a little more than a minute left. Seconds later, in the center of the ring, he landed a multipunch combination, punctuated by a left hook.

Referee Norm Bellieux intervened and waved his arms above his head to stop the fight as Green fell backward onto the canvas. It was the first time in Ward's career that he had scored a knockout beyond the ninth round. The technical knockout came with just 20 seconds left in the fight and Green leading on all three scorecards. Micky Ward, who took more than two dozen stitches afterward, would live to fight another day.

Reggie Green also fought again—four times—beating three nondescript opponents before suffering another, career-ending, 10th-round TKO at the hands of IBF champion Zab Judah, then 25–0, in January 2001.

For Micky Ward, the difference between winning and losing the Reggie Green fight was easily measured: He was offered his first-ever six-digit payday—$100,000—plus $20,000 in training expenses, to fight Shea Neary for an otherwise meaningless title belt sanctioned by something called the World Boxing Union.

It was a deal that came together after multiple other possibilities came and went. Potential opponents who had been considered for Ward had included WBC champion Kostya Tszyu, Mexican legend Julio Cesar Chavez, and Arturo Gatti.

The timing was wrong for Tszyu: Ward was still too banged up from the Green fight to accommodate the champ the following December, when they would have fought as the cofeature on the Fernando Vargas–Winky Wright HBO card. Then, Chavez—maybe the best 140-pound fighter in history—inexplicably lost to Willy Wise.

Gatti–Ward seemed likely for the undercard of a show at Boston's FleetCenter, where Neary was to be matched against Ray Oliveira, but that deal fell apart when Gatti demanded too much money.

Neary, from Liverpool, England, was 22–0, with 16 knockouts, but he had never fought outside the United Kingdom. The biggest name on his resume was probably Darryl Tyson, a well-worn former title contender who had nine losses by the time they'd met. This fight also would be in the United Kingdom, in Kensington, England, and would be shown by HBO.

Despite Neary's unblemished record, Ward felt unusually confident after watching tapes of his previous fights. The so-called "Shamrock Express" was a stationary, full-speed-ahead puncher, as opposed to a stick-and-move cutie, which fit nicely with Ward's style. Ward didn't fear Neary. Indeed, he was confident. His own record was spangled with world-class opponents—guys like Brazier, Warren, and Judah—whereas Neary was, by comparison, a babe in the woods.

"I knew I had more experience than this kid. I knew I'd felt more pain," he writes.[3]

Ward also was motivated when he learned that British bookies had made him a 5–2 underdog.

Neary proved to be skilled and formidable, but he also was wild and reckless, leaving himself open for counterpunches. For that, he paid the price. Dicky told his brother between rounds to look for the knockout. They didn't want the fight to go to a decision in Neary's house.

For seven rounds, the two gladiators stood toe-to-toe, battering one another ruthlessly. HBO's George Foreman opined during the fight that Neary was the better fighter of the two. But with 40 seconds left in round 8, Ward fired a left hook to the body that hurt his opponent and then drilled him again to the same spot. When Neary dropped his hands to protect his ribs, Ward planted a left uppercut on his chin, sending the Brit to the canvas for the first time in his career. Neary got up quickly, but Ward pounced, dropping him again with six unanswered punches, four of them with the left hand. Referee Mickey Vann had seen enough and stopped the fight.

"He's done it again!" exclaimed HBO analyst Larry Merchant with reverence for Ward. "He's done it again."

The fact that he'd won the WBU world title, rather than one of the major belts, mattered little to Ward at that moment. He dropped to one knee, whispered a prayer of thanks, and stood up to celebrate with his brother Dicky, cutman Al Gavin, manager Sal LoNano, his father George Ward, and his girlfriend (and future wife) Charlene Fleming, who kissed him on the lips.

For Ward, the victory meant more than any other to that point. He admitted later that he was choking back tears, as he did his postfight interview on HBO. The title belt from the WBU meant little in boxing's pecking order of alphabet-soup championships, but it meant plenty to Ward, who finally could call himself a world champion.

But the often-bipolar nature of a professional boxing career would continue through Ward's next four fights, beginning with his matchup in August 2000 with Antonio Diaz, a talented California fighter from a well-known boxing family. Only 23 years old, Diaz was 34–2. Both losses had come early in his career, and he hadn't tasted defeat in more than four years, despite facing an impressive list of opponents that included multiple title challengers and former or future world champions. Diaz had held the IBA's version of the 140-pound title since September 1999, and had successfully defended that crown four times.

But no world championship would be at stake for Ward–Diaz. Both men had vacated their titles, rather than accept unsatisfactory offers to face mandatory challengers.

In Ward's case, WBU president John Robinson wanted to bring him back to England to defend against another British contender. Instead, he was offered twice the money—$175,000, by far the largest purse of his career—to stay home at Foxwoods Resort in Connecticut and fight Diaz on HBO. The bout would be the appetizer for a main event between Prince Naseem Hamed and Augie Sanchez.

Team Ward knew in advance that Diaz would be an exceptionally tough matchup—Micky would be a serious underdog again—but that's life for an almost-35-year-old fighter with a 35–9 record. An upset victory would possibly earn Ward a lucrative shot at the top 140-pounder on the planet, Kostya Tszyu, or maybe Arturo Gatti.

He lost a close but unanimous 10-round decision to Diaz. Two judges scored the fight 96–93, while the third gave Diaz the edge by just one point. Diaz then moved up in weight to fight for Shane Mosley's WBC welterweight title. For Ward, it was back to the drawing board to prepare for another rugged Californian, Steve Quinonez, whom he fought nine months later at Foxwoods.

For a fighter who had been through multiple all-out wars, spilled gallons of blood, and suffered broken bones and countless contusions, the Quinonez fight might as well have been a refreshing stroll in the park. With 20 seconds left in the first round, Ward hit the California fighter with one of the best left hooks of his career, then watched him deflate and fold. Just that quick, it was over. It was the first time in more than four years that Ward could remember getting off work early.

In July 2001, he went to Hampton Beach, New Hampshire, to face one of the most colorful and unusual fighters of that generation, Emanuel Augustus (previously known as Emanuel Burton), whose 24–17–4 record couldn't have been more deceptive. Burton was an enigmatic Chicago fighter whose mercurial work ethic—or lack thereof—had led to multiple losses early in his career. By the time he fought David Toledo in 1998, he was 11–12–3. But Augustus not only knocked out Toledo, 25–1–1 at the time, he embarked on a 10-fight unbeaten streak against mostly formidable opposition. Four of those opponents had a combined record of 128–3.

Ward versus Augustus was a 10-round war so spectacular that *Ring* magazine called it the "Fight of the Year" for 2001. Ward won the decision—his second impressive victory in a row—thanks in part to a ninth-round body shot that put Augustus down, and moved on to his next opportunity against former two-division world champion Jesse James Leija.

Ward and his handlers knew in advance that the Leija fight was another one they wouldn't be likely to win on the scorecards. Leija would be fighting in his hometown, San Antonio, Texas, where the officiating and judging regularly stank of hometown cooking.

Referee Laurence Cole unabashedly proved that those fears were well-founded after a left hook from Ward slashed open the eyebrow of Leija, a notorious bleeder, just two minutes into the fight. Cole immediately stopped the action and declared that the injury had been the result of a phantom accidental head butt. A fight that is stopped due to an accidental clash of heads goes to the judges' scorecards. If the fight ends on a cut that was caused by a punch, the injured fighter loses by technical knockout. If a referee isn't absolutely certain the cut was opened by a head-butt, he is obligated to rule that it happened from a punch. That's the rule.

"I knew as soon as I had thrown it that it was a good, clean punch," Ward said later at a press conference. "You hit a bleeder with a hook to the eyebrow and sometimes the tissue just pops right open. That's what happened. There was no head-butt. Absolutely not."[4]

When Ward got back to his corner, Al Gavin was waiting with the expected warning: "This is Texas, Micky. You can't give him anything."[5]

At the end of the fourth round—the round that makes a 10-round fight official—Cole called the ring doctor to Leija's corner to examine the injury. Ward threw his hands in the air in frustration when the fight was stopped and placed in the hands of the judges, two of whom awarded the fight to Leija by a split decision.

Micky Ward was 35 years old and had lost two of his last four fights. Now what?

# 8

# REBIRTH

**A**rturo Gatti was eight months from his last ring appearance and two years from his most recent victory when he returned to action at Foxwoods Resort in Mashantucket, Connecticut, on August 14, 1999, against a fighter who, as HBO blow-by-blow commentator Jim Lampley unapologetically implied, most likely belonged in boxing's "tomato can" category. He was brought in as cannon fodder.

Reyes Munoz was born in Ponce, Puerto Rico, reared in New Jersey, and, by the time he faced Gatti, was working for $12 an hour at a concrete beam foundry in Erie, Pennsylvania. He walked to work every day because he couldn't afford a car. Munoz had won a New Jersey Golden Gloves crown as an amateur and had compiled a respectable 21–3 record, with 9 KOs, in the pro ranks, but his most notable victory had come against a lightweight named Troy Fletcher, who was 13–7–2, with a six-bout losing streak. Munoz's biggest paycheck in boxing had been $800. On this night, against Gatti, he would earn $35,000.

The HBO broadcast crew tried to maintain a semblance of credibility without blatantly confessing that this guy was being served up to Gatti on a platter. Gatti understood that losing to a club fighter at this point in his career would be the death knell, but Munoz was so far from being a threat that the "Human Highlight Reel" couldn't have been less concerned.

Gatti made weight with a pound to spare, at 139 pounds, and stepped onto HBO's unofficial scale a day later, shortly before the opening bell, at 160. The network's veteran ringside analyst, Larry Merchant, tersely noted that an overnight weight gain of 21 pounds was nearly irrefutable evidence that the fighter didn't break much of a sweat in the gym, choosing instead to cut weight at a frantic pace in the final days.

In the end, it didn't matter. Gatti was Gatti, and Reyes Munoz was a guy who worked in a beam plant. To his credit, he nearly made it through the first round. Just before the timekeeper pounded on the ring apron to alert the fighters that 10 seconds remained, Gatti clobbered his opponent with an overhand right, followed immediately by a textbook left hook. Munoz went down, then valiantly stood up again, but his legs wobbled so badly that veteran referee Eddie Cotton immediately stepped between the two men to prevent an involuntary manslaughter—or perhaps a premeditated murder—charge for the promoter and matchmaker.

Munoz exited the arena on a gurney, with a brace on his neck and an oxygen mask over his mouth and nose. Gatti was so clearly concerned that he could barely complete a postfight interview with Merchant. Instead of hanging around to talk to reporters and watch HBO's main event, he followed the ambulance to the hospital and stood vigil until he was sure he hadn't killed someone. Fortunately, Munoz recovered, but he never fought again.

And while the obliteration of an overmatched opponent wouldn't completely restore the confidence of a fighter like Gatti, it had to be regarded as a nudge in the right direction. His three-fight skid had been halted.

For better or for worse, Gatti made a career move after the Munoz victory, splitting from trainers Ronnie Shields, Lou Duva, and Roger Bloodworth—who, friends convinced him, had been too lax, enabling his party lifestyle—and reinstalling hardnosed Hector Rocha, plus his own older brother Joe. Rocha had been an architect of Gatti's earlier success, guiding him to the IBF super featherweight crown and two successful title defenses. After losing to Angel Manfredy, Gatti had replaced Rocha with Shields, Duva, and Bloodworth, who were in his corner for both of the Ivan Robinson losses, as well as Reyes Munoz's near-death experience.

Rocha's task was to reacquaint Gatti with the philosophy that fights are won and lost in the gym, rather than in the arena, on fight night. But discipline and self-discipline are two very different things. Gatti was young, handsome, single, and famous, with a ready roll of cash in his pocket. He loved beautiful women, and the feeling was mutual. And he lived just across the bridge from the greatest party town on the planet, New York City.

"Listen, he was loveable to anybody," said Gatti's close friend and nightlife wingman Mike Sciara in an Internet interview with boxing journalist Ryan Songalia.

> When the girls got to meet him and talk to him, he had that accent, he had the biggest, brightest smile, he had that little-kid look in his eye . . . he just had a good aura around him, no matter who met him, whether it was a young lady, an old lady, an old man, a young man, a kid . . . he just had this genuine aura of quality, or pureness, of being fun. When he walked into a dark room it just lit up. [1]

While those qualities are helpful in a nightclub full of friendly women and bartenders, they're anything but compatible with the training regimen of a world-class fighter.

In *Legendary Nights*, legendary cutman Joe Souza declares that Gatti was a stressful fighter for his trainer Lou Duva.

"I'll tell you, he gave Lou Duva more grey hairs than anything else," said Souza, who staunched the flow of blood in many of Gatti's biggest fights. "But Lou loved him. Lou had a lot of fighters, but he sure as hell loved Arturo. Arturo was one hell of a fighter, and he would never try to let anybody down." [2]

Gatti's next opponent was no tomato can. Joey Gamache was 55–3 and the former WBA champion in both the super featherweight and lightweight divisions. He was 29–0 before he suffered his first loss, a TKO to Tony "The Tiger" Lopez, in a fight that was nearly dead even on the scorecards going into the 11th round. His second defeat had come in a WBA lightweight title fight against undefeated Orzubek Nazarov of Kyrgyzstan, whose record remained unblemished for four more years, until he lost his crown to Jean-Baptiste Mendy in the final fight of his career. His only other defeat had come at the hands of future Hall of Famer Julio Cesar Chavez, who was 96–2–1 at the time.

Gatti's startling 21-pound overnight weight gain, which had turned heads before the Munoz fight, turned out to be anything but an anomaly. He logged in at 141 pounds—the contract limit—when he weighed in for Gamache at Madison Square Garden on February 25, 2000. Twenty-seven hours later, on fight night, HBO's unofficial scales registered 160 pounds—another eye-popping, 19-pound overnight increase. That doesn't happen, trainers insist, unless a fighter has cut a massive amount of weight in a short period of time.

Gamache, by contrast, weighed 146 on fight night—just six pounds heavier than the night before—essentially creating a fight-night mismatch between a welterweight and a super middleweight. If Gamache could take his opponent into the later rounds, Gatti's clear-cut lack of dedication to training was likely to take a toll. Fighters who lose a large amount of weight in the final days or hours usually fade badly. But that didn't happen.

Gatti rolled out the heavy artillery from the opening bell, fighting an aggressive and fearless opening round. With 1:06 to go, he found Gamache with a long right hand that dropped him onto the bottom rope. Gamache got up quickly, but with 40 seconds left, Gatti sucked the air out of his opponent with a body shot and followed with a left hook that landed flush on the chin. Gamache rose on wobbly legs at the count of three, took the rest of the standing eight count, and then, as ringside analyst George Foreman urged him to grab and hold, instead stumbled forward and fought back.

Bad idea. He ate two more massive power shots before the end of the round. The second came just after the bell, earning Gatti a stern warning from ref Benji Estevez while the disoriented Gamache staggered toward the wrong corner.

"How you feel, champ?" trainer Jimmy Glenn can be heard asking Gamache on HBO's broadcast after Gamache found his stool.

"Good," Gamache muttered without enthusiasm.

"You know where you're at?"

"I'm in a fight," he responded.

"Huh?"

"I'm in a fight," he said again, which prompted the ring physician to lean in closer and repeat Glenn's question.

"I'm in the Gatti fight," Gamache told the doctor. "I'm in the Garden."

The answer was satisfying enough to the doctor that Gamache was allowed to return to battle. Thirty seconds into round 2, Gatti buckled him again with another big left to the chin, then pounced with a horrifying right–left combination.

"Gamache's eyes were closed before he hit the canvas," Lampley said as Estevez squatted over the fallen fighter, not bothering to count.

Gamache stayed down for several minutes, surrounded by medical personnel, who were worried that his eyes repeatedly rolled back in his head. The two-time world champion looked as if he had no idea where he was or what had happened to him.

The impact of that knockout was multipronged and historic: The athletic commissions in both New York and New Jersey made a decision to return to day-of-the-fight weigh-ins, rather than giving fighters a full day to rehydrate.

Gamache's promoter, Johnny Bos, accused the New York State Athletic Commission of botching the weigh-in. A lawsuit was filed on behalf of Gamache, which, after 10 years of court battles, was decided in his favor, thanks in no small part to a tell-tale videotape from the weigh-in. The tape, which was played in court, shows that once Gatti stepped onto the scale, the needle rose to the top of the beam, indicating that he was heavier than the contract weight of 141 pounds. With Commissioner Melville Southard looking on from only inches away, Executive Director Tony Russo can be seen touching the scale, moving the counterweight to a heavier position, past the preset weight of 141 pounds. When that fails to settle the needle, Gatti is told to raise his arms, which causes the needle to bounce up and down. While the needle is still in motion, Gatti's weight is announced as 141 pounds. At that point, Gatti steps off the scale, immediately begins drinking fluids, and is hustled by his handlers out of the weigh-in room.

Gamache's handlers immediately raised a protest to Southard and Russo, pleading for Gatti to be reweighed. Russo's responses, caught on tape, were as follows: "Shut the fuck up" and "Stop stirring up shit."

"I don't know anybody outside of the Gatti camp who seriously maintains that Gatti made weight for that fight. They jumped him on and off the scale very quickly," recalled renowned boxing journalist Thomas Hauser. "It seemed pretty clear to me that someone at the commission had been told in advance that there might be a problem, and the response was, 'Don't worry about it.'"[3]

Gamache, who sustained permanent brain damage from the knockout, never fought again. He also harbored no ill feelings afterward toward Arturo Gatti.

"He was a fighter, just doing what he's supposed to do," Gamache said. "The commission was supposed to protect us fighters."[4]

Meanwhile, Gatti's second-straight spectacular knockout victory restored him to the good graces of promoters and TV producers. He had demonstrated resoundingly that he was still a major attraction in the sport.

He fought twice more in 2000, knocking out Eric Jakubowski (20–6) in the second round just 57 days after the Gamache fight and outpointing future world champion Joe Hutchinson (18–0–2) in Gatti's hometown of Montreal in September. With a four-fight winning streak in progress—including three spectacular KOs—Gatti moved to welterweight to face the biggest star in boxing, the "Golden Boy," Oscar De La Hoya.

A dirty little secret about professional boxing—one of zillions—is that some matchups between fighters with marquee names are fully expected to be mismatches from the day the fight is made.

Team De La Hoya regarded Arturo Gatti, a superstar to his fans, as a perfect foil for the "Golden Boy," who by fight night had been idle for nine months and lost two of his previous three fights (albeit to future Hall of Famers who were at the peak of their powers, Felix "Tito" Trinidad and Sugar Shane Mosley).

For the most part, Gatti had made his bones at 130 and 135 pounds, only recently campaigning at 140. The De La Hoya fight would be at welterweight—147 pounds—a natural weight at this point in Oscar's career. Indeed, De La Hoya's plan was to have a fairly easy time with Gatti, then bolt to 154 and try to win another belt there.

What De La Hoya's camp understood was that Gatti almost certainly would bring his usual bravery into the ring and slug it out with an opponent who was bigger, stronger, and probably faster. Not only that, but Oscar's jab was considered a weapon every bit as devastating as his celebrated left hook. A running joke about Gatti was that his face began swelling and bleeding in the dressing room before the fight. Conventional wisdom was that Arturo's courage, aggression, and utter disregard for defense would make him a clay pigeon for De La Hoya, who held a five-inch reach advantage and was 2 1/2 inches taller.

For those reasons, De La Hoya opened as a 30–1 betting favorite in Las Vegas, where the fight would be held. (Gatti loyalists, flooding in from the East Coast on fight weekend, brought in enough late money to lower those odds to 8–1 by the opening bell.) The numbers at the sports books made no difference to Gatti, who would be earning his largest paycheck to date—$1.5 million—to face the most popular fighter of their era. He looked relaxed and confident, as always, as he bounced on his toes, moving toward the ring at the MGM Grand, flanked by trainer Hector Rocha and his brother, Joe Gatti. "Woke Up This Morning," the theme song of HBO's smash-hit series *The Sopranos*, blared from the arena's sound system—a tribute to Gatti's adopted New Jersey roots.

Although De La Hoya had been only a pound heavier at the weigh-in, it became clear during the prefight instructions that he was the larger, stronger man—disadvantages Gatti had rarely encountered in his 37-fight career. What Gatti and Rocha believed was that Arturo would have an advantage in hand speed. That wasn't the case. The 22 minutes in the ring with De La Hoya would be painful and cause Gatti to do some soul searching.

A crowd of 10,000 saw Gatti come out of his corner jabbing with a jabber and hooking with a hooker from the opening bell. The earliest moments of the fight belonged to "Thunder," who got De La Hoya's attention with a flush left hook midway through the first round, the first of several effective punches that would follow.

But with 22 seconds left, De La Hoya made his planning committee seem like soothsayers with a flurry of punches that included a head-snapping left uppercut—a punch that crumpled Gatti to the canvas. Somewhere during that same combination came a blow that opened a two-inch gash under Gatti's left eye, an injury that also began to swell immediately. Gatti got off the deck and finished the round, then plopped onto his stool, where Hall of Fame cutman Joe Souza went to work with adrenaline-laced cotton swabs and a one-pound Endswell—an ice-cold piece of metal used to minimize swelling.

Although Gatti started round 2 with more bad-intentioned haymakers, De La Hoya was emboldened, answering with soul-sucking shots to his opponent's body and head. Oscar threw 42 power shots during the round, landing 32.

Gatti also was scoring with big shots but was discovering that punches that turned out the lights on opponents at 130 and 135 pounds were having little effect on De La Hoya, whose own resume already included encounters with Mosley, Trinidad, Fernando Vargas, Ike Quartey, Pernell Whitaker, Oba Carr, Miguel Angel Gonzalez, and Julio Cesar Chavez (twice), to name just a few. By the third-round bell, most observers already saw the end coming.

It arrived 76 seconds into round 5, when the increasingly swollen and bloody Gatti became "target practice," as HBO blow-by-blow man Jim Lampley put it, for De La Hoya. The "Golden Boy" landed 24 of the 26 power shots he threw, prompting Rocha to leap onto the ring apron and hurl a towel at referee Jay Nady.

Gatti was infuriated when his trainer stopped the fight, but he conceded during his postfight interview with Larry Merchant that Rocha only had his safety in mind. "I could have kept going, but my trainer decided I'd had enough, and I respect his judgment," he said.

The statement turned out to be more magnanimous than sincere. It would be the last time the trainer and the fighter would team up. The next time Gatti would enter the ring—nine months later in Madison Square Garden, against former super lightweight champ Terron Millet—he'd be taking his instructions from another former world champion, Buddy McGirt.

During the six months that followed his brutal knockout loss to Oscar De La Hoya, Arturo Gatti licked his wounds and contemplated his future. His confidence was wavering. He wasn't even sure he wanted to fight again.

When the itch to train returned, he relocated to Vero Beach, Florida. Gatti liked it there—liked the quiet, relaxed atmosphere and the sunshine, each a significant contrast to the New Jersey lifestyle to which he'd grown accustomed. The change suited him.

The other change occurred the day he spotted two-division world-champion-turned-trainer Buddy McGirt at the gym. They clicked immediately and decided to work together. The marriage was perfect. McGirt, a boxer-puncher in his heyday, had captured the junior welterweight crown in 1998, and was building a formidable reputation as a trainer by the time he connected with the warrior known as "Thunder."

Gatti dismissed Hector Roca, the trainer who had guided him to a world championship, two days after his first day in the gym with McGirt. It wasn't personal. It rarely was with Gatti. Aside from understanding Gatti's style and skills, McGirt intuitively knew what was going on in the fighter's head and immediately went to work on the fragile psychology that comes with being a boxer scabbing up from a tough loss. He told Gatti that he could be a champion again and laid out a plan to make it happen.

His newest client could move and had a pretty good jab, McGirt observed. The trainer's goal was to reconvert Gatti into a boxer who wasn't necessarily destined to be in a life-or-death struggle in every fight. The transformation wasn't as difficult as it sounds. Unlike most confirmed brawlers, Gatti *could* box. He knew how to use the ring. His jab was effective, when he used it. The 29-year-old Gatti liked what McGirt was telling him and focused on conditioning and spent fewer nights in the clubs.

In January 2002, the Gatti–McGirt collaboration was unveiled against former IBF junior welterweight belt-holder Terron Millett, a respected opponent who had lost his crown 19 months earlier to undefeated Zab Judah. The other loss on Millett's 26–2–1 record had come in 1995, against Sharmba Mitchell, a future world champ.

In the opening stanza, Gatti bounced on his toes and snapped off jabs. He dug a left hook to the body. Seconds later, a lead right hand—one of Muhammad Ali's favorite punches—found the chin of Millett. When Gatti bobbed and weaved, Millett looked at him like he was crazy—this wasn't the Gatti he had expected—but all he hit was air with most of his punches. Gatti moved side to side in round 2. After Millett clocked him with an uppercut, Gatti went back to shooting his jab, then stepped inside and unloaded. Seconds later, he moved away. Millett stalked, but his movements had slowed. Gatti pounded the body and head. Millett backed up and wobbled. A big left hook in round 3 floored Millett. The game fighter survived the round, but it was obvious that his resistance was weakening. The following round, Gatti cashed in on the preceding damage, brutalizing Millett for almost two and a half minutes before a thudding combination brought the fight to its inevitable conclusion.

Gatti was back.

The talk at ringside was that Gatti had given his best performance in years. But what ultimately would be the cornerstone of his legacy—and his ticket into the International Boxing Hall of Fame—was yet to come: Team Gatti now turned its attention to Micky Ward.

# 9

# "IT'S GOING TO BE A GREAT FIGHT"

Micky Ward had lost the dubious technical decision to Jessie James Leija in his last go-round, a setback that may well have been a career-ender. Indeed, a week before the fight he had declared that he was finished if he lost.

He didn't know it at the time, but losing to Leija turned out to be the best thing that ever happened to him. An impressive performance might have caused Gatti's team to reconsider a fight with Ward. Instead, Ward's performance made them think that their guy could handle the 36-year-old Irishman. He was on the downside of his career, while the younger Gatti was shooting for the stars.

A month later, after a few squabbles, the contracts were signed. Ward would earn $435,000—by far the most he had ever been paid. Gatti would go home with a cool half-million. Arturo Gatti and Micky Ward would fight on May 18, 2002, at Mohegan Sun Casino in Uncasville, Connecticut. Their careers, and lives, would never be the same.

Ward recognized that the fight with Gatti was the most important of his 17-year career. He knew that if he could defeat Gatti, more money was on the horizon. During his training, to improve his stamina, he would spar many rounds before taking a break. And then, instead of the standard one-minute rest, he'd take 30 seconds and get right back at it. His mood reflected the stakes. Ward was cranky, so everyone left him alone.

"It's going to be a great fight," he told the media at a press conference a few days before the bout. "Arturo's a great fighter, a warrior, and a great guy."[1]

At the same event, Gatti concurred. "Micky Ward is a lot like me," he told the press. "He's a warrior. I'm a warrior. When you have two guys like us, you never know what's going to happen. It's like two pit bulls."[2]

As they waited in their dressing rooms, both fighters were confident. Gatti planned to box and shoot his jab. Ward wanted to engage. His goal was to start faster than he had during the Leija bout. Everyone knew that Gatti was the better athlete. But could he stay focused and stick and move? That had rarely been his style before.

Gatti's promoter, Kathy Duva, had been assured by Buddy McGirt that they would box. That's what they had worked on during training camp. No more brawls, she was told.

Ward entered the ring first to the strains of some soft rap. The cheers were loud from a home-turf crowd, many of whom had made the 100-mile-plus drive from Lowell, Massachusetts. His trunks were white with a red stripe. Instead of a standard robe, his shoulders were draped with the jersey of the Lowell Spinners, a minor-league baseball team. The number on the back was 38, a digit his victory total would reach if he was able to defeat Gatti.

Gatti didn't make Ward wait long. He gazed at the ring as AC/DC's "Thunderstruck" echoed through the casino. He stepped into the ring as some of the crowd booed. Gatti smiled and looked over at Ward. He was tanned, ripped, and ready to go.

Referee Frank Cappuccino called the fighters to the middle of the ring and gave them their final instructions. He glanced at both and said, "I leave it with you." Gatti and Ward touched gloves and returned to their respective corners. The crowd began to roar.

No moment in sports can equal those final seconds when two bona fide gladiators stare across the ring at one another, awaiting the opening bell. There is a nervous tension, an electrical charge that tingles throughout the crowd. Sometimes what follows proves unworthy of such anticipation—how could it not?—but when a fight lives up to its hype, the level of drama reaches a unique stratosphere. No one in the arena could have anticipated what was about to happen in those high-voltage seconds before Gatti–Ward I. A fight that would live in boxing lore was a bell away.

Gatti and Ward trade violent, compelling, and dramatic punches on the inside during their first battle.

Ward delivers his textbook left hook to Gatti's liver, forcing Gatti to the canvas.

Referee Frank Cappuccino counts while standing over a stricken Gatti in round 9 of their first fight. Many at ringside figured the bout was over, but Gatti got up and fought back.

"Intimate warfare."

A little more than six months after their first encounter, Ward and Gatti meet again. This time the venue is Atlantic City, where Gatti's marathon training camp will pay off.

Gatti was the sharper man in the rematch. A blistering right hand sent Ward stumbling to the canvas in round 3. He pulled himself up and battled back, even though Gatti's blow had broken his eardrum.

Gatti was ready for Ward's money punch in the rematch. Ward tried and failed to land the same blow that felled Gatti in their first go-round.

To the victor goes the spoils. Gatti poses after winning the second fight by unanimous decision. Before the sweat dried, both men had already agreed to fight again.

Respect and admiration: Gatti (left) and Ward after the second fight.

Primed and ready to go: Gatti and Ward face the cameras prior to their third bout.

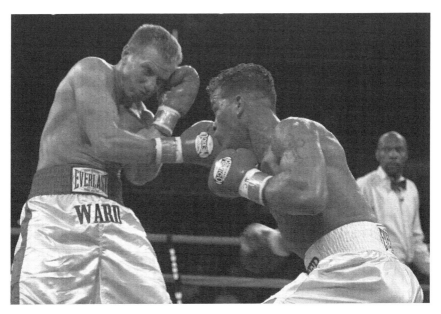

Gatti took up where he left off in the second fight, beating Ward to the punch.

Gatti clips the slower Ward repeatedly with sharp right hands.

Gatti in pain after breaking his right hand in round 3 of his third fight with Ward. The injury would cause a shift in momentum.

Ward lands a blistering right to Gatti's chin. In round 9 of their third fight, a similar blow would send Gatti tumbling to the canvas.

Gatti uses his left to keep Ward at bay, rallying down the stretch to win the third and final bout by decision.

Micky Ward

Arturo Gatti
GATTI vs. GOMEZ

Ward and Gatti, now trainer and fighter, respectively, talk to the press before Gatti's career-ending fight against Alfonso Gomez.

# Part II


# Intimate Warfare

# 10

# BEAUTIFUL, UGLY, AND DANGEROUS

**A**rturo Gatti started the fight boxing, keeping the promise his trainer, Buddy McGirt, had made to promoter Kathy Duva, but he didn't end it that way. At the opening bell, Ward beat Gatti to the center of the ring, but the "new" Gatti bounded away as if to say, "Nope, not yet."

Ward landed a left hook. A few seconds later he did it again. Gatti moved fluidly. He let fly with a right hand that Ward ducked. He jabbed and circled. Halfway through the round, he unloaded a five-punch combination. The last two blows were a left to the midsection, followed by a hook to the head. The hook landed. Ward blinked, already bleeding from the corner of his right eye. Gatti supporters roared. This is what they had come to see. Gatti connected with another shot that knocked Ward back two steps. Gatti was boxing beautifully. His punches were free-flowing. He dug a right to the gut. The work was easy.

Ward stalked the faster Gatti. He ate a jolting combination and pounded his gloves together like a man telling himself to wake up. He pawed at his bleeding eye. Gatti landed another salvo at the bell.

Ward's cutman, Al Gavin, liked to say, "If you can't stop the flow, then you go."

Everyone depended on Gavin, one of the all-time greats, to stop the flow. He never panicked and always knew exactly what to do. Gavin had worked for Lennox Lewis, Junior Jones, Kevin Kelly, and Oscar De La Hoya. He was like a superior athlete who couldn't explain how he did his job so well. He had a feel.

As Ward slumped on his stool, Gavin—68, but extremely spry—went to work. "You're all right," he reassured Ward as HBO's ringside microphones eavesdropped. "It's on the outside."

This was good. If the cut had been above the eye, the seeping blood could have impaired Ward's vision. Gavin wiped it away and applied a cotton swab. He squeezed the cut and coated it with Vaseline. The entire procedure had taken less than 40 seconds. Ward didn't look worried. He felt strong and confident. To a bleeder like Ward, blood was a nuisance, and little more.

Gatti attempted to build off his success of the opening round. He continued to move confidently in round 2. He jabbed and backed up, mixing up his shots. Going into the fight, everyone (Ward included) knew that Gatti had the faster feet. Ward waited, eyeing Gatti, trying to time him. He fired a right that Gatti ducked. Ward chased after him.

Gatti unloaded combinations from different angles that connected. Ward pressed forward, his gloves high, looking to land something significant. He was edging closer, making Gatti work. Referee Frank Cappuccino stepped in near the end of the round. After Gatti dipped low to fire a few body shots, Cappuccino broke the fighters and leaned into Gatti, their foreheads bumping.

"Keep them punches up, brother," he warned.

Gatti said nothing and walked to his corner. He had dominated the first two rounds. Ward had worked in training camp on moving his head, but so far Gatti rarely missed. Ward needed to do something, anything, to change the momentum of the bout.

In Gatti's corner, McGirt complimented his charge on how well he was boxing. But he couldn't shake the memory of a mysterious stranger—apparently a Ward fan—who had passed him in the casino, predicting Gatti would be tagged with a Ward liver shot. McGirt remembered the taunt and warned his man to be careful of such a punch—but also to keep his hands up.

Gatti landed a hard left hook 30 seconds into round 3. Ward then walked into a jab but kept moving forward. He touched Gatti's head with a lead right hand. Gatti moved away, sticking out his jab. He was heeding McGirt's advice to keep boxing.

Ward went to work on the body. Gatti fired punches in combination. Ward landed two more body shots. A few seconds later, a short hook to the ribs connected. Was he finding his rhythm? Gatti moved away, but a subtle change was occurring. Ward opened up some more. His contingent from Lowell screamed as another hook dug into Gatti. A right also landed. Gatti fought back with his own punches to the midsection. That had always been his way. Get hit, but fire back with more punches. A wide, powerful hook crashed home. A couple of uppercuts jolted Ward.

When the bell rang, Gatti sat down heavily on his stool. McGirt asked him what he was doing. Why had he gotten away from boxing? Gatti didn't answer. The trainer told Gatti to stop taking "that body shot."

But what could Gatti do? Ward had perfected the bullet to the liver years earlier. In 1997, Ward was in deep trouble against red-hot prospect Alfonso Sanchez. He had been cut and floored in successive rounds. The shellacking was so one-sided that commentator Larry Merchant remarked that the bout should be stopped. But in round 7, Ward began to throw his left hook with serious intent. A perfect shot to the ribs sent Sanchez to his knees gasping for air. He couldn't beat the count.

Gatti certainly knew this, but his focus seemed to be wavering. His body language suggested pain. He stood and gazed at Ward. Would he go back to boxing or decide to slug it out?

Ward tried to land a sneaky punch a few seconds into round 4. Gatti dodged it. He went back to working his jab. Ward feinted and let fly with a wicked right hand. The punch had missed numerous times during the first three rounds. This time it didn't. Gatti felt it. He backed into the ropes and covered up. Ward went after him, but Gatti stayed aggressive. A hard left knocked Ward back, but only for a few seconds. Blood now was oozing from Gatti's mouth, and his left eye was beginning to swell.

Ward went to the head and body. Gatti absorbed the shots. Both fighters landed heavy left hooks. Gatti landed a vicious shot south of the border that sent Ward to all fours. He vented his frustration, beating a glove against the canvas. Gatti felt he'd thrown a legal punch, but Cappuccino had seen it clearly. He ruled it a low blow.

Ward got up quickly. He had five minutes to recover.

Gatti was scolded by Cappuccino, who said, "You keep doing it, fella." Gatti argued back.

Cappuccino ordered the judges at ringside to take a point away from the disgruntled Gatti. The timekeeper had forgotten to stop the clock when Cappuccino halted the action, and the bell rang. Gatti and Ward touched gloves and walked slowly to their corners.

Gatti shot a hook to Ward's gut a few seconds into round 5. The punch was an inch or so above the belt. He would not play it safe. Being penalized a point meant nothing. War was war. Ward pressed the action. Gatti pounded him with thudding punches to the chin and looked puzzled as his opponent remained upright. What did he have to do to hurt this guy? Ward responded with a beauty of a hook to the side. Gatti retreated, and then, like an Italian sports car running low on gas, slowed down and stopped. He let fly with more heavy punches. Ward was eating three blows to land one. He didn't seem to mind. He was bleeding again from his right eye.

Gatti stopped punching, perhaps to catch his breath, and paid a price. Ward went to town with shot after shot. Gatti teetered on one leg after a right landed. He fought back with a combination. Gatti backed away and landed another salvo of vicious punches. Ward nodded in acknowledgment, then smacked Gatti with a classic combination. He dug another shot to the ribs, followed by a right hook to the chin. A body shot hurt Gatti again. He looked tired. His right eye was now cut. Some of his blood had joined Ward's on the canvas. His early lead was evaporating. Ward had stolen the momentum by forcing Gatti to fight flat-footed.

Buddy McGirt screamed at his fighter between rounds to stop taking unnecessary punishment. Al Gavin told Mickey Ward to aim his punches. For the second consecutive round, his onslaught had sent shock waves through Arturo Gatti's body.

Gatti went back to boxing in round 6. Ward, energized by his success, chased after him. Gatti stuck out his jab and used his legs to avoid Ward. He needed to be more scientific to win, but Ward would have none of it. It wasn't so much a battle of wills as a battle of breeding. Gatti was born to slug, but so was Ward. They were brothers from different mothers.

Gatti was reminded again to box. For once, he wouldn't rebel. He'd follow instructions. In round 7, he skipped away and stuck his left in Ward's face. A combination rocked the bloody Irishman. Gatti mixed up his attack.

Ward landed a strong right. He couldn't match Gatti shot for shot, but he wouldn't stop. Gatti circled, staying on his back foot. His jab was his best friend. Ward received a tongue-lashing from his brother, Dicky Eklund, as he waited for round 8 to begin.

"Bang the shit out of him," the HBO audience heard Eklund implore. "Don't be a punching bag. If you're going to be a punching bag, I'm not going to let it go like this. Fight hard!"[1]

McGirt told Gatti there were 10 minutes left in the fight. He didn't need to remind him of the obvious—that a fight can change in a matter of seconds. Ward went back to the body. He wasn't desperate, but he was punching more. Gatti fought back with purpose. Ward caught him with a left. Gatti landed another combination, but Ward kept coming. He was looking for that one shot that could change things. But could he land it?

With 50 seconds to go in the round, Ward landed a stinging right. Gatti tried to roll with it, but he backed away. Ward forced him into the corner and let his hands go. Gatti took two steps back, as if resigned to what was coming. Ward shot his hook to the liver. Gatti moved away but stopped. It was time to make a stand again. He unloaded. Ward absorbed. Blood was streaming down the side of his face.

Ward strafed Gatti with a powerful combination. Gatti wobbled. Ward was on the attack. He connected with more head punches. Gatti unleashed a vicious combination that Ward swallowed without blinking. The tough-as-nails Irishman fired back, stunning Gatti, who was finding it more and more difficult to keep the onrushing Ward at bay.

The bell sounded, saving him—for the moment—from more thumping punches.

The fight had changed again. Gatti waited for his stool. McGirt screamed in his ear. Gatti looked like he needed the 60-second break.

Ward was already resting. His corner frantically told him to keep it going. Ward shook himself alert and glanced over at Gatti's corner.

The crowd was still buzzing as the bell for round 9 echoed. Ward wasted no time going after the backpedalling Gatti. A right hand found the temple. Gatti held on, but Ward dug two left hooks to the gut. Gatti fought back, but the shots to the midsection had weakened him. He wasn't helpless, but he was close. As he backed away, Ward threw his money punch, the left hook to the liver. Gatti straightened up, took two steps back, and fell to one knee.

Head shots are pretty and crowd-pleasing, but a liver shot has a para-lyzing effect on an opponent—an ache so deep and all-encompassing that his body, from the torso down, becomes nonfunctional, usually for much longer than a referee's 10-count. He cannot breathe, he can't stand, he can't think clearly. Liver shots finish mortal men, but this was Arturo Gatti.

Gatti grimaced and made temporary eye contact with the crouching Cappuccino. He pulled himself up at nine, still in pain, and waited. The crowd rose to a collective one.

Ward waded in and went back to work. Another punch to the ribs connected. Gatti was in big trouble. A follow-up right glanced off Gatti, who tried to crouch. He staggered away like a man leaving the scene of a head-on collision. Ward chased, landing three left hooks and a right hand. Gatti was wobbly but again refused to go down. He found the energy to throw a jab. Ward stalked, then Gatti planted and let go with a hook.

Ward, after firing at least 50 punches in the first minute of the round, was arm weary. He stopped punching. Gatti dug deep and inexplicably started to fight back. He had been in this position many times before, staring at defeat, and miraculously rallied. Where it came from, no one really knew. Could he do it again? He fired a hook that missed, but a three-punch combination didn't.

Ward stood and waited. He raised his arms to protect his chin, so Gatti dug two borderline punches to Ward's body. Ward nodded in appreciation. A few seconds later, an explosive right crashed off Ward's chin, backing him up. HBO's Jim Lampley screamed into his microphone at the stunning turn of momentum.

Gatti followed Ward, with his hands low. The boxer had disappeared. Gatti, the predator, was back. Blood dripped from the cut above his right eye. Another blow drove Ward into Gatti's corner, and the Irishman gulped for air. Gatti followed with bone-rattling punches to Ward's body and head.

With less than a minute to go in the round, Ward went back to his own deep well, halting the onslaught. Both men threw haymakers, but Ward's landed first, stopping Gatti in his tracks. Ward knew what to do next. He uncorked another body blow that made Gatti pause, then, sensing an opportunity, followed with an adrenaline-primed uppercut and right hand. Gatti fell into a clinch. He looked exhausted. Ward snarled and unloaded, sending Gatti back to the ropes, where he grabbed Ward and held on. The respite was temporary. Another burst of blows banged off Gatti's head.

He should have gone down—almost anyone else would have—but he didn't, and Ward pounded him until the bell rang.

As Gatti collapsed onto his stool. McGirt tried to shake him up. "Listen to me," McGirt said. "I'm not going to let you take this punishment!"

Gatti glanced to his left, but McGirt wasn't finished "Look at me, Arturo," he demanded. "Tell me something!"

Gatti said nothing. He probably wished the fight was over. His body was limp—posture uncharacteristic of one of the ultimate Alpha dogs in boxing history.

In Ward's corner, Gavin leaned close and said, "This guy's done." Dicky added some words of support.

Both fighters had shown a deep-rooted intestinal fortitude, something that can't be taught. You have it or you don't. Beautiful, ugly, and dangerous.

Then a strange thing happened. A few seconds before the final round was to commence, it looked like the brutality had stopped. People began milling around in Gatti's corner. The HBO crew surmised that his corner had called off the fight. Confusion reigned.

A relieved Ward shot his hands into the air in jubilant victory . . . until Cappuccino bellowed that the bout wasn't over.

The bell for round 10 had already sounded, but the round didn't begin for another 30 seconds, as the referee straightened out the misunderstanding. Meanwhile, Ward and Gatti forced their exhausted brains and spent bodies to refocus on the task at hand. There were three minutes of hell to go.

The 10th and final round was all about Gatti. He jabbed and moved side to side until Ward tagged him with a sweeping left. Gatti took the shot, bent over, and uncoiled with an uppercut, followed by a four-punch combination to Ward's head. A light right hand missed, but a left hook landed clean.

Ward wasn't doing much. Gatti clipped him with a lead right. Ward was being backed up for the first time in 20 minutes. Gatti kept punching. Ward started to fight back. The last 20 seconds harkened back the days of legendary heavyweight champion John L. Sullivan. Both fighters were exhausted. Defense was an afterthought. They stood in the center of the ring and swung freely—until Gatti stumbled into Ward.

The bell sounded, ending the skirmish. Gatti walked to his corner and was coaxed to sit down. Ward paced. They awaited the judges' decisions. Opinions varied on who won. Many thought Gatti had built up a substantial lead. Others felt Ward's rally and knockdown was enough to earn him the nod. The scoring was divided. Judge Frank Lombardi scored the bout 94–94, a draw. Richard Flaherty tabbed Ward the winner by a single point. Steve Weisfeld's scorecard had a margin of two points.

Ward had said he'd retire if he lost. Gatti was in line for another shot at a title if he emerged victorious. Ring announcer Mark Beiro paused before bellowing, "The winner by majority decision . . . Irish Micky Ward!"

Gatti's head dropped a little. He looked at the canvas and turned around and walked toward Ward. Dicky picked up his brother, who raised his clenched fists to the sky. Gatti was the first to congratulate him.

Gatti's low blow and the knockdown by Ward in the ninth round—which all three judges scored 10–8—won him the fight.

"Arturo's a gentleman," Ward said during HBO's postfight interview. "He's a great fighter. He didn't have to prove nothing to no one tonight. He's proved over the years what he can do."

"He's a very tough guy," Gatti said. "I hit him with some good shots. He kept getting stronger every round."

HBO's Larry Merchant waited until the end of his in-ring interview with Ward and Gatti to ask the inevitable question: "Do you guys want to do this again?"

"I would love to," said Gatti. "I would love to get a rematch."

"If we can do it, we'll do it," Ward agreed.

Ward shook Gatti's hand, and the deal was sealed long before any negotiations began.

They had hammered one another with 521 punches, but the blood brothers wanted a sequel. In their minds, little had been settled. Ward had earned the victory, but there was no loser that night in May.

In a little more than six months, Ward and Gatti would meet again—and both men could barely wait.

# 11

# "LET'S DO IT AGAIN"

Micky Ward told his representatives, Lou DiBella and Sal LoNano, that he wanted $1 million to step into the ring with Arturo Gatti again.

A million to a guy with 11 losses on his record? You bet.

As the winner of the first match, Ward was in a good bargaining position. The public at large craved a second fight. Ward and Gatti wanted it. Everyone was on board, so it was conceivable that Ward would receive a bigger payday. A few members of Ward's team wanted him to push DiBella, who was set to earn a ton of money, out of the negotiations, but Ward wouldn't do it. He was grateful to the promoter who had landed him the first Gatti fight. Ward had always been a loyal guy. He was fine with whatever DiBella earned.

Gatti wanted the second fight badly. He wasn't thinking about money, although he, too, would earn $1 million. His mind was fixed on the opportunity he'd blown in the first go-round. He hadn't listened to Buddy McGirt: He'd fought Ward his own way—with abandon—and had lost the fight, and he was devastated and filled with regret.

"I wish I didn't stand in front of him the way I did," Gatti lamented at a news conference in Atlantic City a few days before the rematch. "Sometimes the warrior comes out in me and wants to stay there and trade punches. I don't know why I do that."[1]

Many did know why. Gatti was a battler. He was at his most dangerous when hurt. He wanted to fight, not box. The theme going into the second match was whether, unlike the first bout, he could stick to his game plan—Buddy McGirt's game plan. Could he stay disciplined?

He likely figured he couldn't knock out Ward, so Gatti was determined to train even harder for the sequel. He'd use his legs to stay away from the dangerous Ward and make him pay when Ward got too aggressive. Plans always look good on paper—"Everybody's got a plan until they get punched in the mouth," Mike Tyson famously told the media before a fight—but Gatti was focused.

Meanwhile, to the victor goes the spoils, and Ward was definitely enjoying himself. He was suddenly a star, a status he never expected to achieve, especially at 37.

The rematch would be held on November 23, 2002, at Boardwalk Hall in Atlantic City. The fight was a sellout.

Both fighters were confident.

"Micky Ward is a warrior," said Gatti in a September press conference in Boston. "I'm fighting a guy like me. He's a great fighter. I want to thank Ward's camp for giving me this opportunity. I felt our first fight I could have won. I am going to win on November 23."[2]

"It's going to be a great fight again," Ward said. "Styles make fights. We have the same styles, and neither of us wants to go backwards. Win or lose, we'll fight like men. I'm going to get in the best condition." He added, "Arturo thinks he's going to win. I'm confident that I'm going to win. When it's over, I'm not going to lose."[3]

In one sentence, Ward had summed up what makes boxing a mesmerizing sport: Two fighters, on a collision course, have total faith in their own abilities and—even more important—their own will to win. Each believes he possesses a bottomless well of determination that, when it is needed, will be there—and be enough—when he needs it. Both have tortured themselves in training camp for weeks—sometimes months—to prepare for this specific opponent. Both have been honed to a razor-sharp mental edge by a team of trusted boxing experts. Neither believes he will lose the fight—yet, one of them will.

In the case of Gatti–Ward, there was no smack talk. There were no taunts. The affection between the two men was obvious. It was all about respect.

In the rematch, it was Arturo Gatti who made his way to the ring first. Some of the sold-out crowd at Boardwalk Hall—his "home arena"—reached out and patted him on the back, but he didn't acknowledge them.

His focus was steady. He stepped through the ropes and bounced around the ring.

Ward entered seconds later to the strains of Whitesnake's "Here I Go Again," a perfect song for the moment. The rivals were doing it again, and the boxing audience was already roaring. Spectators wanted another great fight, a replay of that first epic war. Was it possible? How could it be? And how could it not? It had been six months since their first brutal encounter, barely enough time for the blood to dry.

Ward was wearing the number 9 on his white boxing trunks, in honor of baseball Hall of Famer and Boston legend Ted Williams. Gatti wore blue trunks. Both stood 5-foot-8, and each weighed 142 pounds.

After touching gloves and returning to their respective corners, Gatti winked at McGirt. Gatti was just as impatient as the crowd for the fight to begin. Twice he stepped toward the center of the ring, anticipating the bell. Referee Earl Morton held out his arms to hold him back.

"He told me, 'Coach, we got this,'" remembers McGirt of Gatti in *Legendary Nights*.[4]

Diagonally across the ring, Ward stared straight ahead and waited for his cue. He was 1–0 against Gatti and had no reason—none at all—to think the rematch would end with a different result. In mind, body, and spirit, he was ready.

As expected, Gatti came out boxing. Ward followed him, stalked him, throwing more jabs than usual. Gatti jabbed as well, moving in and out. Thirty-eight seconds into the round, he countered a lazy Ward left with a blistering lead right hand over the top. The punch didn't hurt Ward but foreshadowed what would come moments later. Gatti repeated the feat a couple more times before the bell.

Gatti had dominated the first round, and McGirt loved what he was seeing. "Very good," HBO's microphones heard him say as Gatti sat on his stool. "Everything is beautiful. Keep doing what you're doing. Stay low and you can do this all night."[5]

In Ward's corner, the mood wasn't as upbeat. "Hands up! You're letting him beat you to the punch every time," Dicky scolded. Ward nodded without a hint of concern. In most of his 50-plus fights, he had rarely won a first round. He needed to warm up.

Ward connected with a left hook seconds into round 2. Gatti grabbed him, missed a right, and moved away. Ward looked energized; he moved inside and nailed Gatti with a liver shot. A right hand also landed.

Gatti went back to jabbing. He stayed low and found Ward with a hard right uppercut. He was still beating his rival to the punch. Gatti avoided a Ward blow and went back to doing what had worked so well in the first fight. He banged a vicious one–two off Ward's midsection. Gatti backed away and shot another left to the face, then just missed a lead right at the bell.

Ward had a cut on the bridge of his nose when he returned to his corner, where Dicky yelled in his ear, "You got to keep your hands up! Don't let this guy take advantage. Come on!"

"He's looking for the right hand over the top," McGirt told Gatti. "Keep dropping those right hands to the body. Give me speed and double up on that jab."

Gatti threw the first punch in round 3. Ward blocked it. He jumped in and caught Gatti with a left hook that drew some "oohs" from the crowd.

Seconds later it was Gatti's turn to connect. He slid to his left and backpedaled. He grabbed Ward. Was he laying a trap? A hard right landed again. Gatti was sharp and landing at will. Ward was tough and absorbing the blows. He'd been born with one of the best chins in the fight game, but sometimes, as Gatti well knew, a punch doesn't have to land on the chin to do damage.

Forty-three seconds into the round, Ward lost his balance and fell forward. Gatti planted his feet and unloaded a bone-rattling right hook. The punch caught Ward behind the left ear. The pride of Lowell pitched forward, grabbing at the ropes to stay upright. His left knee touched the canvas for a knockdown.

Gatti had moved away at impact, watching Ward much like a home-run hitter after connecting with a mighty blow. Morton pointed him toward the neutral corner. The crowd was on its feet. And so, somehow, was Ward. He wobbled and glanced at Gatti. After reassuring Morton that he was okay, he staggered to his right to face Gatti's bull rush.

But he wasn't okay—not even close. With two minutes left in the round—an eternity in boxing—Ward tried to protect himself by throwing up his arms. Instinct took over.

Gatti flailed with heavy shots to the head and body. Many missed, but a few landed. Ward tried to fight back. Another punch landed in the same spot that had produced the knockdown.

A minute and 40 seconds were still left in the round. After separating from a clinch, Ward tried to step forward, but his right leg refused to cooperate. He looked like a man who needed to call a cab at 2 o'clock in the morning. Ward badly needed a ride home, and Gatti was trying to send him back to Massachusetts.

In a show of bravado, Ward pounded his own midsection, challenging Gatti, who paused, probably figuring his nemesis had lost his mind. But he admitted after the fight that even a wounded Ward was dangerous.

Instead of going to the midsection, Gatti let fly with another heat-seeking right, a blow that landed like a ton of bricks on Ward's head. Ward staggered again but didn't fall. Was he out on his feet? How could he not be?

"That punch woke me up," Ward says in his autobiography. "No shit! I got knocked out cold and then got a wake-up call in the same round."[6]

Amazingly, after moving a bit, his legs steadied. A minute remained in the round. Gatti connected with another hard shot. He glanced at Morton, as if to say, "What have I got to do to knock this guy out?"

Ward responded with a blow that stopped Gatti's onslaught, digging his Sunday punch to the body. Gatti curled as if he had been shot. This bullet had hurt. He backed away. They traded combinations in the last 30 seconds. At the bell, Ward celebrated by pounding his gloves together. He had survived and still had time to mount a comeback.

The fight doctor was in Ward's corner within seconds. He asked the fighter if he was okay.

"Yeah, I'm fine," replied Ward without hesitation. The doctor was satisfied.

"Ice, ice . . . fuckin' ice!" Gatti screamed at one of his cornermen.

How a trainer chooses to use the one-minute break between rounds can be the difference between winning and losing for his fighter. McGirt, the former world champ, had been on the other end for much of his life and understood when and how to push his man's buttons. He knew when to motivate, when to encourage, when to whisper, when to erupt.

"Listen to me," said McGirt to Gatti. "This is yours. Go out and use the jab. Go back downstairs. The right hand over the top is going to work, baby."

Everyone expected Gatti to go for the kill in round 4, but the boxer returned. Gatti circled and jabbed.

Ward switched to southpaw and connected with a left to the chin, which made Gatti hold on. Ward dug another hook to the liver. Gatti fought back, but now his left eye was spurting blood. Ward connected with two stinging left hooks. Gatti pawed at his eye like a wounded animal, then unloaded an uppercut and a right to the heart.

The crowd at the Boardwalk thundered as the bell sounded.

"Take a deep breath Arturo!" McGirt yelled. "Suck it up. Here we go. They don't have to be hard shots to the body, Arturo."

"Much better," Eklund told his brother across the ring. "That's it. You took his best shots, now it's your turn to retaliate. Let's go! He's dead tired!"

"He's worn down right now," cutman Al Gavin agreed.

Gatti clipped Ward with a right hand to the left ear to open round 5. Ward pursued. He banged to the body, but Gatti nullified the impact by bending forward. He held Ward. Seconds later, he was back working his jab, moving in and out. Ward was reaching—a no-no in boxing—and paying for it. Gatti landed a three-punch combination. He was controlling the fight by boxing. Could he keep it up?

In the last 30 seconds of the round, Ward rallied. Gatti could have bounded away but instead cracked Ward's head with a right.

Gatti used the ring in round 6. He was beating Ward to the punch. Ward was making him work, but Gatti was in excellent shape. He dodged and ducked as Ward looked to counter. It wasn't happening—yet.

"You're boxing beautiful," McGirt told Gatti in the corner.

Ward probably figured that Gatti would tire. Was he right? He eyed the ring canvas, possibly pondering what to do. He had to understand, at that point, that he was substantially behind on the scorecards, but he also knew he had rallied before. Many times before. It wasn't out of the question. It never was with Ward.

Gatti went to the body and head in round 7. Ward answered with a stinging left hook, but Gatti danced away like a man without a care. He stabbed Ward with his jab. Gatti was on a mission, and Ward couldn't figure out how to get him out of his rhythm. Gatti now was dominating and enjoying himself. A vicious uppercut shook Ward again. Gatti watched his rival closely after he nailed him with a crunching right hand at the bell.

"Stay focused!" McGirt shouted, understanding how a boxer's focus can fade without notice. "We got nine minutes!"

Ward stumbled and sat down in his corner, where Dicky, the master motivator, threatened to stop the fight.

"I'm good!" Ward protested through the chaos.

Gatti continued to execute his plan in round 8. He jabbed and backed up. He sent Ward back a step with a short right, then rattled him with a big left hook at the bell.

"He's going to get desperate. Don't go for the knockout!" McGirt warned, understanding his fighter's attack-dog instincts.

"Ward is willing to take five punches to land one," said former heavyweight champion George Foreman, who was calling the action for HBO with Jim Lampley and Larry Merchant.

"You can win this fight!" Gavin implored in Ward's corner, while, at the same time, Dicky again was threatening to stop it.

"I'm all right, Dicky. C'mon!" Ward argued, leaning to his right for a glimpse at Gatti. He knew his brother was only trying to motivate him. Both were frustrated.

There were six minutes to go, and everyone in the arena knew one thing: Ward needed a knockout. The crowd screamed as both fighters rose for the start of round 9, each masking the agony with his best poker face.

They began the round with an exchange of jolting uppercuts. Arturo Gatti skipped around the ring. He stayed low. Micky Ward chased, trying to land something hard. Gatti threw combinations. Ward ate them. Gatti could have moved. He could have continued to pile up points. That's what McGirt and Kathy Duva would have preferred. But after getting hit with a right hand, he pushed Ward into the ropes and opened fire. The crowd loved it. This is what they had paid for. Ward returned punches in the last 10 seconds. He connected with a right, but the shot lacked power.

"He's three times tireder than you've ever been!" Dicky exhorted as his exhausted brother gasped for breath. "He's dead tired!"

McGirt acted the cheerleader in Gatti's corner, but also urged caution. Barring a mistake, this fight was won. "Listen to me!" he shouted. "Don't fall into his trap. Three minutes! Can we do three minutes?"

"Yes sir!" responded Gatti emphatically.

Instead of touching gloves at the start of the final round—tradition in the sport—Gatti and Ward embraced in respectful acknowledgment of the ordeal each had forced upon the other. Has that ever happened before in boxing history? Each man then took a step back and quickly stepped forward, attacking. Gatti moved away, then connected with a stinging right hand. He grabbed Ward. He landed a big left hook. He was trying his best to do what McGirt had told him.

Ward tried to punch back but couldn't stay with Gatti, the boxer. He landed a left hook that knocked Gatti back a few steps, bringing back the warrior he'd come to know. Gatti stopped boxing, stayed in the pocket, and punched. Ward fired back as the crowd stood and yelled.

The gladiators, in defiance of their utter exhaustion, were going at it hard. Blow after blow landed. At the bell ending the bout, Ward looked at the canvas, resignation on his face. Gatti jumped on the top ropes and shot his right hand into the air.

Gatti and Ward embraced again, seeming more like brothers than adversaries.

Judges George Hill and Luis Ramirez had Gatti winning the fight, 98–91. Joseph Pasquale scored it 98–90. Their scores were on the money. Gatti had landed more than 90 punches.

Gatti was jubilant, Ward extremely disappointed. Merchant asked why the outcome had been different in the sequel. Gatti said, "I listened to my trainer. I used my legs. I boxed the way I should have in the first fight. I didn't lose a lot of energy. I stayed in front and moved my head. We worked on staying low.

"He had a hard time landing his body shot because I was low," he continued. "It gave me an opportunity to move around him. I was in great shape. I think I landed more punches than the first fight.

"Micky Ward is a very tough guy," said Gatti about the fight-changing knockdown he scored in the third round. "He was never the same. It was a pretty clean shot. I was timing him. No doubt about it. I knew he would get up and finish this fight," he said. "There aren't many guys like Micky Ward."

Ward offered no excuses. "He fought a good fight, and a smart fight," he said. "I give him all the credit in the world. He's a great fighter and a good guy. It was his night tonight. He's a strong guy," he continued.

Merchant asked if he'd fight Gatti again. Ward shrugged. "If we can get it together again, I'll give it one more shot." he said.

Gatti agreed.

"Well, I have to thank God we're both healthy," Gatti said. "He fought a great fight tonight. It's 1–1 now, so a third one? I wouldn't mind."

Gatti tapped Ward and put out his hand. Ward shook it, twice. Both smiled. The stage was set. They would meet for the final time a little more than six months later. And, like their first two bouts, the third wouldn't be lacking in action, drama, or pain.

# 12

# BLOOD AND GUTS

Once more, for all the glory.

The stage may have been set, but the money wasn't. Ward wanted another million—like he had earned for the Gatti versus Ward II, not the $800,000 originally offered. He told everyone he was retiring.

Boxing isn't always about talent. Selling tickets is a must. A 10-round fight between a couple of guys that many believed were past their fistic primes—neither holding a championship belt—with 18 losses between them? That's not a typical recipe for a box-office bonanza. But this was Gatti–Ward III. Tickets went faster than pork chops in a dog kennel.

Gatti's promoter, Main Events, eventually added an additional $300,000 to Ward's purse, tacking on 25 percent of the gate. It was the least they could do. After taxes and expenses, Ward would clear $750,000. The site once again would be Boardwalk Hall in Atlantic City.

"There's no one tougher than Micky Ward," Gatti declared in a pre-fight press conference. "I wasn't sure I wanted to fight him again. But I gave him my word, and here we are."[1]

Ward meant it when he said the third Gatti fight would be his last. He had fought for next to nothing many times in his 50-fight career. His gross for the three Gatti fights would exceed $2 million. He'd earned every penny. Not bad for a guy who, not so long ago, was part of a crew that paved roads. Ward wanted to win the third fight badly. He was determined to stroll into the sunset with one more victory over his now-friendly rival.

But Gatti also was confident. He knew what he had to do. Knowledge is power. His right hand, broken when he floored Ward in the second fight, was feeling pretty good. According to trainer Buddy McGirt, he'd shown up one day with a unique way of protecting the limb.

"Arturo had gone out and bought one of those small seats from a 10-speed to protect his hand," McGirt said with a chuckle.[2] The makeshift pad worked. Gatti trained without incident.

Gatti's team expected Ward to make some adjustments, based on how easily their charge had won the second fight. Ward agreed that he had to move his head more and avoid following Gatti around the ring. He'd counterpunch.

McGirt was more pragmatic. He knew what kind of fighter his guy was going to encounter. "Micky Ward isn't going to come out and fight like Muhammad Ali or Sugar Ray Robinson," the former champion told the assembled media.[3]

Most boxing people assumed that Gatti, younger by seven years, would repeat the strategy he'd used to win the second fight. He would showcase his superior boxing skills and avoid the Ward left hook to the ribs like the proverbial plague. It wasn't as if Gatti could forget that hook; under his ribcage, compliments of Micky Ward, was a cyst, a lasting reminder of the damage the Irishman could inflict.

No surprise, the fight was sold out. Boxing fans knew what they were getting. There was no quit in either man. Many were hoping for a rerun of the first bout, which had been picked as "Fight of the Year" by boxing experts. Everyone was ready.

Ward stood quietly in his corner. He again wore a baseball jersey with the number 39 on the back, the number of wins he'd have if he defeated Gatti for the second time. His hometown contingent roared as he made his made way to the ring.

The Jersey City fans screamed in response as Gatti, their adopted hometown hero, stepped through the ropes.

"Ten rounds of boxing for the unofficial, but undisputed, blood-and-guts championship of the world," bellowed ring announcer Michael Buffer.[4]

The fighters touched gloves as referee Earl Morton recited instructions they'd heard hundreds of times.

Round 1 began as the last fight had ended, with Gatti boxing. He jabbed and moved. Ward had promised he would be aggressive. He wasn't about to break that promise. He stuck out his left and followed with a right to the point of Gatti's chin. Gatti bounced off the ropes. Ward wasted no time going to the midsection. He dug a right to Gatti's ribs and let fly with his patented left hook to the side. Gatti moved away quickly, seemingly reminded of the continuous danger the Irishman represented. Gatti landed a right hand that stopped Ward's momentum.

Gatti knew he couldn't stand in front of Ward. Two minutes in, Gatti connected with a blistering left hook. The blow caused a small abrasion above Ward's right eye, and Gatti made the injury a target for his right hand.

HBO's microphones heard McGirt gush with praise as Gatti sat down.

"Beautiful, beautiful!" the trainer said. "He's trying to throw you off by throwing a right hand."

In Ward's corner, his big brother reminded him of what he had to do. "Mick, you gotta throw," said Dicky. "You're letting him get off every time. You threw the right hand once, and it was perfect."

Ward had likely figured that punching in volume might mess with Gatti's rhythm. The scheme had merit, but how could he do that for the entire fight? Gatti knew what he had to do—box—but history had proven that when Gatti was provoked, he'd set his feet and fight back. It was only a matter of time.

Gatti went to work in round 2, blistering Ward with left hooks to the body and head. When Ward whiffed on a right hand, Gatti skipped away like a kid in a candy store. Now he was boxing sweet, and Ward was having a hard time finding him. Gatti dug a left and right to the midsection. Everything was working.

Ward fought back with his own shots, but Gatti nailed him with another hook to the body. Gatti stabbed Ward with his left. He was dominating the round. Ward was doing just what he didn't want to do—following Gatti and not throwing punches. His nose was also bleeding.

Gatti met Ward in the center of the ring in round 3. He wasted no time getting off first. His left was paying dividends. When Ward blocked it, he went to the body with his right. A combination made Ward take two steps back. Ward finally landed his money shot to Gatti's side. Gatti pounded his gloves together and got back up on his toes. He zinged Ward's face with a four-punch combination. Gatti was lively and full of energy.

Ward caught him with a blow to the chin. Gatti moved his head. He stepped in, punched, and backed away. Ward was eating punches as he backed into the ropes. Gatti was beating him up. Ward ran into a left hook. Gatti was back on his toes like a show pony, and Ward had no answers.

"Very beautiful," McGirt gushed in Gatti's corner. "Okay listen, let's go back downstairs again. He's going for the feints to the body. Like I told you, he's going to counter with that hook. Just stay low."

"Relax, relax," Dicky implored. His brother's face was a mess. Ward's left cheek was swollen. His nose wouldn't stop bleeding. He took an extra swallow of water and looked at his brother.

Gatti seemed to already have the fight in the bag. But boxing is filled with dramatic developments, and round 4 would be talked about for years.

The start of the round was a repeat of the previous three. Gatti punched and slipped away. He tattooed Ward's face with a combination. Then, 28 seconds in, everything changed. Gatti ducked a Ward jab and attempted to land a right uppercut. The punch came up short. It banged off Ward's hip.

Gatti flinched and jogged toward the ropes. Ward quickly attacked. He fired a left hook, followed by a right hand. Both connected. Gatti was in pain. He tried to hold on, but Ward pulled away and landed a vicious left hook to the belly. Gatti backed away but didn't punch back. He finally threw out a few left hands like wounded prey attempting to fend off a predator. It didn't work. Ward stalked him. He worked the head and body. Gatti held his right near his chin, then finally let it go. It landed on Ward's side, but the look on Gatti's face was revealing. Clearly he had broken his hand for the second time in six months.

Ward attacked with renewed vigor. He was back in the fight. Gatti backed away and tossed out his left. There was nothing on his punches. He was trying to survive. Ward landed two left hooks to the head and body. A sweeping right knocked Gatti back toward the ropes. Ward leaned on Gatti and unleashed five consecutive left hooks. Four landed.

Gatti got on his bicycle. He moved away. His greatest asset, his heart, was being tested once again. The last two minutes must have felt like an eternity. He backed into the ropes and ate another right. Gatti fought back. He landed a vicious five-punch combination. Four of the blows were left hooks. The crowd was now in a frenzy. Gatti fired his injured right again, but this time he recoiled in pain, then fell into a clinch.

Ward seized on the lull to go back on the offensive. Three left hooks and a long right hook landed. Gatti fell into the ropes. He held the right in check and fired a left, stopping Ward in his tracks. Gatti was a one-handed fighter, but an effective one. Ward fought back as 15,000 fans stood, screaming at the roller-coaster action.

HBO's cameras zeroed in as Gatti sat in his corner, leaning into McGirt. "My hand . . ." he said to his trainer covertly.

"Huh?" McGirt answered.

"My right hand."

"What do you want me to do?" the trainer asked.

"I got to keep going."

"Listen," McGirt barked, "this is what you got to do. Use that jab. Keep it working! Don't stay inside and take body shots."

Gatti moved side to side in the opening seconds of round 5. Would he stay away or ignore the pain and throw punches? First he jabbed, as Ward walked him down. Gatti's legs were working, so he used them. Forty seconds into the round, he landed a couple of right hands. A stinging shot to the belly straightened Ward up.

Gatti wasn't grimacing anymore; the injured hand had gone numb and he was fighting, back to beating up the equally determined Ward. He went to the ribs and bounced away, seemingly back in control of the bout.

Ward was looking for one big shot. He fired the haymaker with a little more than a minute left. It missed by inches. Gatti connected with a right that created a cut over Ward's left eye and stayed on the attack. A huge left hook landed flush, but Ward took it without a flinch. As Ward pawed at the blood streaming into his left eye, Gatti pummeled him. Many were right hands, but it no longer seemed to matter to Gatti.

An accidental low blow by Gatti suspended the violence momentarily, and then Ward landed a hard right to Gatti's chin. He stumbled slightly, but before Ward could follow up, Gatti moved to his right and let his left hand go. The shot landed on Ward's left cheek. He blinked and countered. Gatti punched back as the bell rang.

"He's fighting you with one hand," said Al Gavin while working on the slash above Ward's left eye.

Dicky then taunted his sibling, hoping to extract some fury: "You're gonna let a one-handed fighter beat you?"

Ward grimaced and said nothing.

McGirt reminded Gatti about Ward's lethal left hook. "He's going to drop it on you," he warned.

Gatti used his legs in round 6. A left hook found pay dirt. Ward followed, clipping Gatti's chin with an inside punch. Gatti feinted and bounced on his toes. He was back in control of the fight. If his broken right hand was bothering him, he wasn't letting on. McGirt had told him to fight smart, and Gatti was listening. Ward didn't accomplish much for most of the round, but he was dogged in his pursuit. He took in a big gulp of air halfway through the round. He let go with a right hand over the top that found Gatti's chin.

Gatti kept shooting his jab and firing shots downstairs. Ward's basement had been his favorite target in all three fights. He even used his right. The punches weren't as hard as usual, but he was throwing them anyway. With less than a minute to go, Ward pounded Gatti's body. He fired a shot to the head as his hometown fans cheered. Gatti went back to moving side to side, but in his heart he liked action. He landed a stinging right uppercut.

Ward followed as usual. Gatti connected with two left hooks. The heat was his, until another dose of drama stunned everyone in attendance. With five seconds to go in the round, Ward fired a sneaky left hook, leaned to his left, and let fly with an overhand right. The blow sent Gatti crashing to the canvas. He got up at three and peered at Ward as if to say, "How'd he do that?"

The bell sounded. Morton pointed Gatti to his corner.

"You gotta watch out for that right hand!" McGirt scolded. "You gotta move to your right more. Keep the left hand out in front of you."

The ringside doctor shined a flashlight in Gatti's eyes and asked if he was okay. Gatti nodded.

"You have to put on the pressure, bang-bang," Dicky told Ward. Ward had done it again. He was back in the fight. Could he capitalize?

Ward fired a glancing combination and dug a hook to the belly. Gatti had stopped moving. He stood in front of Ward and punched back. Boxing smart was a strategy that had gone out the window. It was time to fight. They were like two gunfighters squaring off in the middle of the street.

Ward blocked Gatti's hooks, but not a three-punch salvo to the head and body. A Ward right bent Gatti in half. Ward found his chin with another right. There were still two minutes left to go in the round. Gatti let his hands go, but his left eye was bleeding. The crowd was in a near-frenzy as both fighters pounded one another.

Was it survival or instinct? When Gatti paused to catch his breath, Ward would throw punches. A hellacious counter left hook by Gatti had Ward staggering. Somehow he stayed upright. He fired back the best he could, but Gatti was pummeling the courageous Irishman. With 48 seconds to go in the round, Ward found the strength to bounce on his toes but looked exhausted. The fresher Gatti spanked him with another combination.

Ward dug deep and went to the body. Quitting wasn't an option for either man. They'd go out on their shields—or in boxes. It was that simple.

HBO's cameras captured the drama.

"Look at me" said Dicky to Ward. "Deep breaths, deep breaths."

Ward's left eye leaked blood. His cheekbone was swollen. There was a red smear below his nose.

"Beautiful round, beautiful round, baby," said McGirt in Gatti's corner. "We got nine minutes."

"I knew my soldier had a little more bullets in his gun than Micky," McGirt would say 11 years later in *Legendary Nights*. "Micky was still Micky, but his punches weren't as crisp, and the pressure wasn't as constant."[5]

Ward fired a looping right hand in round 8. Gatti grabbed. Ward kept moving forward. Two right hands and a left hook to the body caused Gatti to back away. Remarkably, Ward was coming on again. Gatti stabbed him with his jab. Ward hadn't been able to find Gatti's ribcage with his money punch. He was still trying. Gatti was doing everything in his power to stop the blow from landing. He kept his right elbow plastered to his side. Gatti backed Ward into the ropes and banged home a right.

Ward was probing with his left and gulping air. He tried a sneaky shot that missed. Gatti made him pay. He landed two left hooks and a right. Another blow knocked Ward sideways. Now it was Gatti's turn to be in control.

"Ninth round," said Dicky as Ward peered at Gatti.

Perhaps Ward was thinking of the first fight, when a knockdown in round 9 had won him the bout. He could do it again if he could get Gatti into position.

Gatti boxed. He feinted and jabbed, and unloaded stinging punches. Ward punched the body. A right hand was a little short. Gatti moved away. After a clinch, he landed his own left hook to Ward's side. The jabs kept tattooing Ward's misshapen face. Another combination landed. They touched gloves after the bell sounded.

"Use your legs, but let your hands go!" shouted McGirt over the roaring crowd. "We got to close the show big, but no slugfest."

"Last round of your career," Dicky reminded his brother.

Ward stood and looked at Gatti. Both men smiled. They had once been rivals, but now they were blood brothers in intimate warfare. Only they understood what they were made of. The mutual respect was obvious as they embraced warmly in the center of the ring.

And then, it was back to trying to knock one another's heads off.

Ward let go with a winging right. Gatti dodged it and moved side to side. Ward needed a knockout to win, but it was Gatti who unloaded. An inside hook wobbled Ward. Gatti rattled him with an uppercut, but the man from Lowell knew only one way to fight. He would keep coming forward. It didn't matter that he couldn't see out of his left eye or that his eyesight was playing tricks on him, making everything fuzzy.

Ward admitted later that he was, quite literally, seeing three Gattis in the ring. The condition would last a year after the bout, but at the time nothing else mattered except winning. He'd fight to the end, attacking the one in the middle.

Gatti continued to throw punches. His broken hand connected numerous times. With a little more than a minute to go in the fight, Ward finally caught Gatti with a staggering left hook. Ward went for it again. A long right thrown from the other side of the ring landed. Gatti looked hurt, but two counter uppercuts forced Ward to back off.

"At this point, now, you're Arturo's team, and you love him, and you want him to succeed, but now you've become friends with Micky and his team, and you love him, too, and now you don't want to see anybody get hurt," says Kathy Duva, Gatti's promoter, in *Legendary Nights*. "The emotions going into the last fight, and that last round, were so different. We started out when it was us against them. By the time it ended, it was just us."

The last 40 seconds were all about guts. The pair stood toe-to-toe, raining punches on one another. Both landed thunderous head shots—a proper send-off for their incredible trilogy.

"Oh, my God," gasped famed trainer Emanuel Steward, who was working the fight for HBO. That expression of pure awe seemed completely involuntary—not for the benefit of network microphones—from a man who, until that moment, probably thought he'd seen everything in boxing and suddenly realized he had not.

The mutual slugfest continued until the final bell sounded. Exhausted, Ward and Gatti hugged again, relieved that the most exciting 30 rounds in boxing history were over.

Eleven years later, Ward talked about his final embrace with Gatti for *Legendary Nights*. "We came together and hugged," Ward recounts, pausing as he watches a replay of his embrace. "I love ya man . . . y'know?"

The judges had Gatti winning the fight by scores of 96–93 (twice) and 97–92.

"I know what type of man Micky Ward is," said Gatti in the ring during a postfight interview. "I knew he was coming in tonight to fight the best fight of his life. If it was anyone else, they would have quit. Micky Ward is unbelievable. He's got heart—and for someone who wants to retire, he fought a hell of a fight."

"He caught me with some good shots early that threw my equilibrium off," Ward said as Gatti listened from a few feet away. "He hurt me early, not real bad, but enough to get me a little dizzy. I just couldn't get untracked after that. He fought a great fight. I take my hat off to him."

They shared a water bottle as they were being interviewed. Ward was asked by Larry Merchant if his legacy would forever be tied to his fights with Gatti. "Yeah, probably . . . most definitely. And I'll stay friends with him for life. That's just the way it is."

While Ward kept his promise and retired, Gatti fought on. They would reunite four years later, with Ward as Gatti's new trainer.

# Part III

# Blood Brothers

# 13

# FRIENDS

The relationship between two boxers who have forced one another to that ledge at the end of the world—a secret place that few will ever see—has been compared to men who survived the battlefield together. Whether they liked or hated one another during the heat of battle, they cannot stop themselves from falling into an embrace when it's finally over. The sheer intensity of the experience seems to merge their DNA, creating a bond that is the closest thing to blood brotherhood.

The truth is, Arturo Gatti and Micky Ward barely knew one another before they met in the ring for the first time, and, by necessity, they built emotional walls to keep one another out during their epic three-fight series. For 30 rounds, they literally wore one another's sweat, blood, snot, and saliva. They felt one another's hot breath and smelled one another's bodies in a way that even the most intimate of lovers cannot match. Each man spent every ounce of his energy, strength, and sheer will trying to vanquish the other, firing artillery shells that, by all reason, should have left any opponent writhing and twitching on the canvas. And yet, in all three fights, the other man was still standing, staring defiantly through swollen eye slits when the final bell sounded.

Incomparable moments such as this are when boxers inevitably fall in love with one another forever. They forgive most, if not all, of the nasty, often vicious things they might have said about one another—or directly to one another—in advance of the fight (although Gatti and Ward, both class acts, never derided or disrespected one another).

There are exceptions—Joe Frazier, for one, famously never forgave Muhammad Ali for calling him an "Uncle Tom," and Marvin Hagler was still refusing to pose with Sugar Ray Leonard decades after their fight—but in boxing, enduring grudges are rare. Graziano and Zale, Louis and Schmeling, Saddler and Pep, Robinson and LaMotta—almost every duo that has been linked by a series of bloody battles in the ring have become friendly, in a permanent state of mutual admiration, in retirement.

Ward and Gatti were never bitter rivals—each was a nice person, not given to the angry rhetoric that precedes most titanic matchups—but they waited until the final punch of their spectacular trilogy had been thrown before they finally became friendly. That's a necessity of the sport.

Their hospital story has become part of boxing lore: Ward was transported by ambulance from the arena to Atlantic City Medical Center to be stitched up, X-rayed, and run through a precautionary CAT scan. As he lay on a gurney, waiting for treatment, Ward's doctor poked his head around the corner and said, "Hey, someone wants to say hello."

"He drew back the curtain, and there was Arturo, waiting for the same sort of postfight cleanup," Ward remembers. "The first thing he said—and this will always stay with me—was, 'You okay, brother?'"

"Even now, after all these years, it gives me goose bumps just thinking about it," he continues. "He didn't make any jokes, didn't say anything about the fight or the crowd—not right away. He wanted to know if I was all right. I knew then that I'd made a friend for life."

Ward describes himself as being "very different from Arturo outside the ring,"[1] but he says their boxing bond made them the closest of friends and brought them together in unusual ways.

In his autobiography, Ward recounts being awakened from a deep slumber by a middle-of-the-night phone call from an officer with the Port Authority Police Department in New York. Arturo had been in an automobile accident. He'd fallen asleep while driving through the Holland Tunnel. The officer said he was okay—just a little banged up—but could use a friend, and they had found Ward's number in Gatti's cell phone and wanted to know if he could come help his friend out.

Ward said that he'd love to be of assistance but that he was in Boston. He passed along the number of a New York friend who also knew Gatti, who stepped in to help that night.[2]

Middle-of-the-night phone calls weren't unusual between Ward and Gatti in the years following their third fight. " We both kept odd hours, so

I'd call him late sometimes," Ward said. "It's funny, when we'd be together, we'd talk to each other, and people would be like 'What are they talking about?' Like, we understood each other, but people were like, 'What the hell are they talking about?' We had our own little language."[3]

Ward also remembered multiple times when he'd be out with friends who would begin reminiscing about the trilogy and invariably ask, "What's Gatti really like?"

"Great guy," Ward would always respond. "Here, you can talk to him yourself."

Then Ward would hit the speed dial on his cell phone, Gatti would answer, and he'd be passed around the table, or put on speaker, so everyone could chat with the "Human Highlight Reel."

"And he'd do the same damn thing to me when he was out," Ward said. "The thing is, no one could really understand what Arturo was saying, with that squeaky voice and the Italian-French accent, all delivered at machine-gun pace.

"Not that I'm the most eloquent guy in the world, but we understood each other. Always had, always would."[4]

# 14

# REUNION

**M**icky Ward joined a very small fraternity when he retired from boxing after his third fight with Arturo Gatti. He was one of those rare birds who apparently walked away from the spotlight with nary a glance in the rearview mirror.

It's not difficult to understand why a boxer almost invariably makes a comeback—even multiple comebacks. There are multiple reasons, each one as alluring as the next.

Consider first that the vast majority of those who rise to the higher rungs of professional boxing have clawed their way out of difficult circumstances. They oftentimes are the products of dysfunctional situations at home—usually exacerbated by some level of poverty—and grew up in dangerous neighborhoods, where fighting on every street corner was a rite of passage. For most of them, boxing became the most important thing in their lives, first as a survival mechanism and then as a heightener of self-esteem among peers.

And then, all of a sudden, the boxer wakes up one morning and discovers he is known. He is recognized on the street, at restaurants, and in the aisles at his local supermarket. He drinks free in local taverns. Children and their parents want his autograph, and beautiful women suddenly find him attractive. This is multiplied exponentially when he begins fighting on television against other well-knowns. Suddenly, the cheering throngs grow larger, and the media attention becomes more intense.

The paydays get much, much bigger—large enough that the fighter no longer has to work a day job to pay the bills, finding time before and after for training. They are suddenly flush with cash for months at a time and brimming with optimism that the next big check—bigger than the last one—is coming soon. They move into larger homes, drive expensive cars, and stay in luxury hotels on the promoter's dime. When the money starts to run out, they fight again, refill their bank accounts, and the party begins anew. As long as they keep winning and remain relevant, all is well.

But few professions are as fickle and unforgiving as professional boxing, where the positive reviews from a fighter's first 20 or 30 victories can turn ugly after just one or two losses. And then, abruptly, the joyride is over. A former top contender, even an ex-world champion, abruptly becomes a "gatekeeper," a "stepping-stone," for the sport's young up-and-comers. Darwin's law of natural selection prevails, and the former Alpha dog suddenly discovers that he is, once again, just another marginalized member of the pack.

The money and fame evaporate. Those legions of "friends" dwindle. The bright lights grow dim. Life becomes bleak and cold when the once-glaring spotlight begins to flicker. Depression often sets in. And, inevitably, a predictable thing happens: Old injuries begin to feel better. A tired body becomes rested. The bills stack up, and the hunger returns. And the fighter begins to believe—almost always erroneously—that he's got two or three good fights left in his aging body and that some unworthy young chump is wearing his old championship belt. Another factor driving a fighter to mount a comeback is love. It's inconceivable for most people to think what it would be like to give up something that has defined you at an age when most folks are hitting their professional stride. Plus, the idea of fighting again for 10 or 12 rounds to earn the kind of money that would amount to a year's worth of paychecks at a construction site, warehouse, or gym—well, it certainly beats working.

Micky Ward felt every bit of that the first time he retired. Remarkably, he experienced little or none of it after hearing the final bell of the third Gatti fight.

"When my brother was done with that fight, he was done, period," Dicky said. "I told him, 'That's it, Mick . . . one more punch could be no more punches.' And he knew what I meant.

"I walked into the gym one day and caught Micky sparring with my nephew [Sean Eklund], and I hollered at him: 'Micky, what are you doing? Get those gloves off!' Sean was unloading on him, and I said, 'Get the hell out of there—I'll do that!'

"Micky didn't really have any real withdrawal pains at all after he retired, but most guys aren't that way," Eklund said. "It's sad that people want to keep putting old fighters out there and make them fight. I'd rather collect cans on the street than do that."[1]

Ward went back to driving his uncle's steamroller, paving streets and parking lots. He stayed connected with boxing as a boxing coach at the gym he opened after his career, making appearances at area boxing events, and, ironically, joining the entourage that walked Arturo Gatti from the dressing room to the ring for Gatti's remaining fights.

When Gatti beat Ward in the rubber match of their trilogy, he was a month short of his 31st birthday, and still one of the hottest commodities in the game. Seven months later, he was back at Boardwalk Hall to fight Italian star Gianluca Branco, 32–0–1, for the vacant WBC super light-weight crown. He won the belt with a 12-round unanimous decision and successfully defended the title by knocking out Leonard Dorin (22–0–1) in two rounds and former champion Jessie James Leija in five.

Gatti then put his WBC strap on the line against the number-one pound-for-pound fighter in the world, Floyd Mayweather Jr., who was 33–0 and, at age 28, in his physical prime. (More than a decade later, he would still be fighting and was still undefeated.) Mayweather battered Gatti in an uncompetitive fight, and the title changed hands via a retired technical decision (Mayweather led by eight points on all three score-cards) when Gatti's corner kept him on his stool at the beginning of the seventh round.

Remarkably, Gatti had one more good one left in the tank: He moved up to the welterweight division and won the vacant IBA championship with an 11th-round technical knockout over Denmark's Thomas Dam-gaard, who brought a 37–0 record into the ring that night at Boardwalk Hall. That would be the last hurrah for the "Human Highlight Reel," who was TKO'd in nine rounds by Carlos Baldomir in July 2006.

Gatti wanted one more fight. Buddy McGirt, who had trained him for four years, disagreed. He advised Gatti, 35, to retire. The former cham-pion ignored him, so McGirt quit. Gatti told his manager, Pat Lynch, the same thing, but this time he added a caveat: If he looked bad, even if he won, he'd retire, but who would train him?

A week or so later, as Gatti languished in Lynch's office, the topic came up again. Gatti mentioned that it would be great to have Ward as his trainer. Lynch liked the idea and called Ward. Within seconds, the former rivals, now close friends, had agreed.

"I wasn't going to teach him to fight," says Ward in *Legendary Nights*. "I was there basically to motivate him, get him going. I'm not going to teach him how to throw a left hook, or a right hand."

"C'mon, he's a lot better than me," adds Ward.[2]

The press loved it. The reunion was something right out of Hollywood, but movies don't always have happy endings. Gatti faced fringe contender Alfonso Gomez on July 14, 2007. He was expected to win but was stopped again, this time in seven rounds.

A sad photograph from that bout—an image so often seen in a ruthless, survival-of-the-fittest sport—shows Gatti, boxing's ultimate warrior, on his hands and knees with a waterfall of blood draining onto the canvas from a severely torn upper lip at the end of the fight.

"He was just stronger than I was," a battered Gatti told Max Kellerman afterward, fighting back tears on HBO. "He was a hungry fighter, a young fighter. I came in thinking I could outbox him, but the ring kept getting smaller and smaller against a bigger man. I don't belong at 147, and I can't make 140 anymore, so that means, hasta la vista, baby."

Gatti and Ward embraced when the interview concluded. Gatti then leaned into the arms of Amanda Rodrigues, the Brazilian beauty he married that same year.

# 15

# AN ENDURING MYSTERY

The last bout of Arturo Gatti's career—that decisive loss to the much larger, much younger, far less talented Alfonso Gomez—was the only time Amanda Rodrigues ever saw him fight. He was 35 by then and riddled with injuries from nearly 20 years of warfare—it was time to go—but, predictably, Gatti never felt comfortable outside the ring, the gym, or the bright lights.

He tried to replicate those bright lights with night life—something he'd done for much of his adult life. Gatti loved bars, dance clubs, strip joints. In fact, Gatti's longtime friend, Tony Rizzo, said Gatti told him he met Rodrigues in 2006, at a New Jersey strip bar called the Squeeze Lounge, where she was working as an exotic dancer. Although multiple employees of the Squeeze have verified working with her, Rodrigues disputes that she was ever an employee. (There also is no record that she was ever employed by the establishment.)

And she has a very different version of her first encounter with Gatti—a story he also occasionally told: They met while walking their dogs near his home. "I remember when I find out he was a fighter, I told him, 'Oh . . . I thought you was even a movie star . . . but not a fighter,' because he was so cute," Rodrigues recounts in a *48 Hours Mystery* report. [1]

Few women would argue with that assessment. Even with two decades worth of ring scars, Gatti remained strikingly handsome and charming, and the fairer sex swarmed around him like honeybees. Nonetheless, less than a year after meeting Amanda, he produced a bottle of champagne, dropped to a knee, and asked her to marry him. "I think it was one of the most beautiful moments of my life," she says. They were married at the Grand Canyon in 2007.

She was just 21, and Gatti was already a father by then. Sofia Bella Gatti, born in March 2006, was his daughter with former fiancée Erika Rivera. Rivera told the *New York Daily News* that Gatti's new bride was so consumed with jealousy that she forced Sofia Bella out of his life.

"Amanda wanted to meet me, and after, she told him: 'You cannot see your daughter,'" Rivera relates. "She was holding him back. How could you do that as a mother? Children are innocent."[2]

Amanda gave birth to Arturo Gatti Jr. in October 2008, and, by all accounts, the former fighter was over the moon about his baby son. Little Arturo gave him a new reason to be in love with his life. That, perhaps more than anything else, is why most people who knew him best remain adamant that Arturo Gatti's mysterious death on July 11, 2009, could not possibly have happened the way Amanda Rodrigues said it did.

Others weigh in during the same *48 Hours Mystery* report.

"I never believed that he did that—that he took his own life . . . never. Everything was going good for him," Micky Ward says. "He had a son that he loved to death. He had a daughter that he loved to death. Two kids. He wouldn't do it. No way. I don't see it."

"His son meant the world to him," claims his friend, ringside photographer Tom Casino. "If you didn't know that his son meant the world to him, you didn't know Arturo Gatti."

"I didn't believe it was a suicide," declares Fabrizio Gatti. "I believe my brother got murdered. And you know what? Nobody's gonna change my mind."

The mystery of how and why Arturo Gatti died on July 11, 2009, may well endure until the end of time. It is mired in confusion and suspicion, beginning with eyewitness accounts of what reportedly was a turbulent final evening with his wife.

What apparently is not in dispute is that Gatti's body was found on the floor of the two-story room they had been renting at a luxury resort in Ipojuca, Pernambuco, in northeastern Brazil, where he, Amanda, and 10-month-old Arturo Jr. were vacationing. Amanda's bloody purse strap, snapped in two, was found nearby. Amanda told police her husband committed suicide by using the strap to hang himself from the staircase above. Brazilian police initially arrested her for murder, theorizing that she had used the strap to strangle her inebriated husband to death.

A great deal—and very little—has been clarified since. According to Amanda, the couple reportedly had planned the trip as a sort of second honeymoon with the hope of working out problems that were threatening their marriage—one of which may have been Arturo's worsening dependence on alcohol and drugs. It was not a new problem for Gatti, who, by his mid-20s, already had been convicted of drunk driving charges in three states. He lost his driver's license for 10 years. Gatti also had been arrested more than once in Miami for brawling with police and had been sued on another occasion for a 2009 fight in Fort Lauderdale that left a man brain damaged.

Their relatively short marriage had been stained with at least one documented episode of domestic violence, an incident that had occurred while they were vacationing on the Hawaiian Island of Maui. Amanda, who was pregnant with Arturo Jr. at the time, confirmed that they had a terrible fight that day but later denied that Gatti struck her.

Life outside of the limelight didn't suit the ex-champ, his wife said.

"He got depressed. He didn't know what to do. He started drinking hard," Amanda says. "There was the man I fell in love [with]—the funny, romantic, lovely husband and father—and there was this person who would change when he was drunk. He would become aggressive, messy . . . he was a completely different man when he was drinking."[3]

Tony Rizzo states that the union had never been a good one and the abuse was two sided. Rizzo claims that Amanda once hit Gatti over the head with a broom and insists that he saw his friend sporting black eyes— apparently unrelated to his profession—on multiple occasions. Rizzo attributes those injuries to the volatility of Amanda. Amanda denies that charge, saying she never struck her husband but admitting to throwing things at him.

Tom Casino, Gatti's friend and photographer, holds a much different opinion. "She tried to help him," Casino says. "I was there when she tried to help him."[4]

Rodrigues had threatened him with divorce on multiple occasions and, at one point, obtained a restraining order to keep him away.

A text message from Rodrigues to Gatti uncovered by *48 Hours Mystery* reveals her anger and disgust: "For me, you are an embarresment [*sic*] inside and out of the ring," she wrote to him. "Wake up, looser [*sic*]. No one is [jealous] of your fucked-up life!!!"

But in June 2009, just before their fateful trip to Europe and Brazil, Gatti drew up a new will, leaving nearly everything—an estate worth millions—to Amanda and their newborn son. Rodrigues holds that document as proof that the couple was trying to revive their struggling marriage, but many in Gatti's inner circle regard it as further evidence that she was little more than a gold digger and grounds for suspicion that she somehow is responsible for his death.

What hasn't been disputed is that Gatti was drinking heavily on the last night of his life, at a night club in the Brazilian resort town of Porto de Galinhas, and that he had been arguing with Amanda. Rodrigues said the evening began with a family dinner at a pizzeria and moved to a watering hole, where Arturo became drunk and mean. The fight started when an annoyed Amanda announced that she was going back to the hotel.

Police reports, based on eyewitness accounts, state that Gatti threw Rodrigues to the ground, causing injuries to her arm and chin. Gatti then reportedly left the area with Arturo Jr., who was in a stroller, but returned a few minutes later. At that point, according to police, the angry crowd began throwing things at the former three-time world champion, and witnesses said he was struck in the head with a rock and then a bicycle. Gatti fought back, reportedly against four men.

Amanda returned to the hotel. Gatti and their son showed up a short time later, with Gatti bleeding from the back of the head and the shoulder, she says, and at that point he noticed her own injuries.

"He said, 'Who did that to you?'" Rodrigues tells CBS reporter Erin Moriarty. "And I said, 'You did this, Arturo.'"

That, she declares, is when she took their son upstairs to bed. "And before I go up the stairs, he look at me. He was sad," Rodrigues tells Moriarty. "He just say, 'So I guess it's over, huh?' And I look at him and I say, 'It's over.' I couldn't take that anymore."

That's where the demise of Arturo Gatti dissolves into one of the most perplexing mysteries in the annals of sport or, for that matter, crime.

How is it possible that Amanda Rodrigues, who weighed little more than 100 pounds, could strangle a three-time world champion boxer to death, even if he were extremely drunk? Why would the famously happy-go-lucky Arturo Gatti, a multimillionaire who, by all accounts, was head over heels in love with his 10-month-old son, commit suicide? How could Amanda have spent 10 hours in the same space with Gatti's dead body before noticing he was dead—the explanation she offered investigators who wondered why she hadn't called for help much earlier?

The story Rodrigues gave police, and also Moriarty, is that she woke up the next morning to feed Arturo Jr., went downstairs, and saw her husband lying on the floor, which, she said, was not an unusual sight after a night of heavy drinking. She assumed he was sleeping and chose not to disturb him.

She said she came back downstairs two hours later, still upset and ready to say good-bye. "When I touched him, he was cold," Rodrigues tells Moriarty. "At that time I knew something was wrong. I wanted to believe he was just passed out, so I start shaking him, calling his name, saying, 'Arturo . . . I forgive you! Please, wake up!' Then I open the door and said, 'My husband is dead! My husband is dead! Please, someone help me!'"

She says she saw the broken purse strap next to his body and knew immediately that Gatti had killed himself. Brazilian police didn't think the crime scene matched her story and arrested her for murder.

Although family members and close friends reject any possibility that the notoriously exuberant Gatti took his own life, there is evidence that he had attempted suicide more than once. A former live-in girlfriend told a Canadian news documentary program, the *Fifth Estate*, that Gatti "attempted suicide by overdosing on cocaine, alcohol, and prescription drugs" in 2005. Hospital records from New Jersey confirm that he arrived at the emergency room in an "unresponsive state" and tested positive for both cocaine and alcohol.[5]

The same news-magazine show interviewed Mario Costa, a longtime Gatti friend, who recounted an incident in 2004, when the fighter had paid a late-night visit to his home. "He says, 'Please give me [your] gun,'" Costa said. "I was afraid. I had my gun there, but I told him, 'I don't have my gun.' . . . I believe if I gave him my gun that night, he would probably blow his head off right in front of me. That's how bad he was."

Amanda Rodrigues sat in a Brazilian jail for nearly three weeks until an autopsy report concluded—controversially—that Gatti had, in fact, taken his own life by hanging himself with his wife's purse strap. Police concluded that he hanged himself in the apartment early on July 11, from a wooden staircase column that was about seven feet off the ground. He stood on a stool and kicked it out from under him, police said. The autopsy report said Gatti was suspended for about three hours before his body fell to the floor.

But those findings were unsatisfactory for Gatti's friends and family.

"Arturo Gatti never would have killed himself," said his friend Ivan Robinson, who fought Gatti twice. "He was a fun, happy, fightin'-his-ass-off guy. Outside the ring he was the most-pleasant, most-respectful, most-loved. He'd give you the shirt off his back. Arturo didn't kill himself. She killed him."[6]

Gatti's former managers, Pat and John Lynch, were of the same mind. They hired their own investigators to take another look at the evidence. The 300-page report filed by those private detectives concluded that Gatti had been murdered.

In August 2009, shortly after Gatti had been buried in Montreal, his family had his body exhumed so a second autopsy could be performed. Those results, released in 2009, were inconclusive but did not rule out the possibility of homicide, and the Canadian coroners found that the investigation by Brazilian authorities had been incomplete.

"The conclusion of the Montreal pathologists to the effect that there is no clear evidence of foul play in Mr. Gatti's death means I cannot dismiss the formal conclusions reached by the authorities of the country where it occurred," reported Jean Brochu, Quebec coroner. "The methods used by the Brazilian investigators in examining the scene of Arturo Gatti's death can raise doubts, and so the [coroner] believes that the circumstances of death cannot be determined with certainty."[7]

In 2012, a follow-up report by Moriarty came up with its own verdict: "The more we investigated the case, the more we discovered that most of the rumors about Arturo Gatti's death were, in fact, rumors and nothing more," Moriarty writes, continuing,

> One of our producers, Josh Yager, tracked down the taxi drivers and spectators in the Brazilian resort town of Porto de Galinhas who saw Amanda with her husband the night of his death. They confirmed that Arturo Gatti, drunk and depressed, had gotten into a fight that evening and was hit and injured in the back of his head by a stranger. There was blood in the cab that Gatti took back to the condo that night.
>
> While there is little question that the initial Brazilian police investigation into Gatti's death was poorly conducted, forensics and tests

done on the boxer's body also support Amanda Gatti's innocence. Gatti was found on the floor after the purse strap he had used to hang himself broke. His body had the kind of lividity, or pooling of the blood, known as "boots and gloves," that usually only occurs when a body is hanging for a substantial period of time. There was no sign that Arturo Gatti had been drugged, nor is there evidence that anyone else entered the condominium at the time of Arturo's death. There was also no evidence that Amanda Gatti had any contact with so-called hit men.

Instead, the evidence shows that Arturo Gatti had been in an emotional downward spiral for months. Years of brutal matches had left him in constant pain. He was taking medication and drinking excessively, and often got into fights. In one altercation in Florida, Gatti hit a man so hard, he allegedly left him with serious brain injuries. Even Gatti's own brother, Joe, believes that Arturo, at such a low point emotionally, finally did what he had threatened to do in the past and killed himself.[8]

Whether Arturo Gatti took his own life or was murdered is a puzzle that has driven a wedge between those who were closest to him.

"I'm not even talking to my family, not because I'm choosing sides, but because I wanted to see [Arturo] Junior," Joe Gatti told Keith Idec of *Boxing Scene* in 2010. "That makes me on [Amanda's] side, I guess. I don't know, but I don't think she did it. What do you want me to do, crucify the lady? I can't."[9]

Anna Gatti, sister to Joe and Arturo, expresses exasperation with Joe in the same article: "I don't know what's going on in Joe's brain," she said. "He doesn't know [Amanda]. He never met her [when Arturo was alive]. I'm sorry to talk about my brother that way, but he was jealous of Arturo from day one, from when [Arturo] won the championship. So that's what it is—jealousy—and it's sad to say that."

Gatti's mother Ida also has told the media that she believes her son was murdered. "They should be ashamed," Joe Gatti relates. "They should be ashamed of what they do. They know that Amanda did not kill Arturo, but they still want to throw it in the street and throw little Arturo Junior in the street with her. It's unbelievable."[10]

Since July 2009, Amanda Rodrigues Gatti has been telling anyone who will listen that she had nothing to do with her husband's death. Nearly three years later, authorities are beginning to hear and believe her.

Family members waged a two-year war over Gatti's estate, accusing Rodrigues of wielding undue influence concerning the new will the fighter signed just weeks before his death, leaving everything to his wife and baby son. The family maintained that Gatti's true wishes had been established by a will he had signed in 2007, just before he married Rodrigues, but no signed copies of those documents were located.

In December 2011, a Montreal probate judge ruled in Rodrigues's favor, finding that Gatti's new will was valid and that Gatti had signed it voluntarily, free of undue influence. The estate, originally valued at $3.4 million, went entirely to Rodrigues, who reportedly cleared $2 million by the time the probate process was over.

Gatti's daughter from his previous relationship with Erika Rivera, Sofia Bella, will receive a college fund and trust account that Gatti had previously established for her.

Rivera is another who can't buy the notion that Gatti may have taken his own life. "Bullshit," she says. "He could get a little bit crazy, he was very superstitious, but suicidal? Never. He was a free spirit who loved life."[11]

Rivera filed a wrongful death lawsuit against Rodrigues in New Jersey. The case was dismissed for lack of jurisdiction but could be refiled, either in Montreal or Brazil.

"I thought she'd be in jail by now," says Rivera, a chemical engineer who designs explosives for the U.S. Department of Defense. "And if she won't go to jail, we'll take away the money. The only way this gets settled is with her not getting one red cent."[12]

Rodrigues originally moved to her native Brazil with Arturo Jr., but in a 2013 article published by Toronto-based *Global News*, she confirms that she has returned to Montreal, where she has opened Boutique AG— the Amanda Gatti Boutique—on trendy St. Denis Street.

"I've learned how to love Montreal," she told the publication.[13]

# EPILOGUE

Micky Ward was one of the six pallbearers who carried Arturo Gatti's casket on July 20, 2009, in Montreal. After spending a private moment standing over Gatti's body, he did something that might seem inappropriate in any other context: He delivered a left hook to Gatti's casket.

*The Fighter*, starring Mark Wahlberg as Micky and Christian Bale as Dicky, was a hit at the box office and critically acclaimed. Bale won the 2011 Oscar for Best Supporting Actor, and Melissa Leo, who played Alice Eklund-Ward, matriarch of the large family, won for Best Supporting Actress. The film was nominated in five other categories, including Best Picture, Best Director (David O. Russell), Best Supporting Actress (Amy Adams as Micky's wife, Charlene), Best Original Screenplay (Scott Silver, Paul Tamasy, Eric Johnson, and Keith Dorrington), and Film Editing (Pamela Martin). Similar honors were bestowed by the Golden Globes, the Screen Actors Guild, the American Film Institute (AFI), and the British Academy of Film and Television Arts (BAFTA).

Among those who gave the movie a thumbs up were Ward and Eklund, although both admitted it was difficult, at times, to see the family's warts exposed on a 22-by-52-foot screen.

Eklund, whose battle with drug addiction is a centerpiece, has just one issue with the filmmakers. "There's a scene in the movie when they've got me jumping out of a second-story window to get away from the cops," he says in an interview on the *Ringside Boxing Show*. "In real life, it was actually a third-story window . . . and I didn't land on no bag of cans when I hit the ground, neither."[1]

Their seven sisters had their own objections, Ward and Eklund have said. "Some of them didn't like the way they was portrayed—all loud, and with the big hair," Dicky says with a laugh. "But, then, you're not gonna make our seven sisters happy, no matter what you do. Ain't gonna happen."[2]

The irony of *The Fighter* is that the story ends before the Micky Ward–Arturo Gatti trilogy—the best part of the story, Ward has said. That, coupled with the sensational story of Gatti's life and career, and the enduring mystery of his death, left a door open for *Can You Hear the Thunder*, a sequel of sorts. Wahlberg (who is not part of the cast) is an executive producer; Jerry Ferrara, who made his bones in the HBO series *Entourage*, was cast as Gatti.

# AFTERWORD

## Arturo Gatti and the Hall of Fame

### John J. Raspanti

**A**rturo "Thunder" Gatti's boxing career was loaded with more "ooh!" and "aah!"moments than five or six fighters put together. A number of his bouts were like roller-coaster collisions—leaving both Gatti and his opponent a mangled mess.

This certainly doesn't sound like a ringing endorsement for a Hall of Fame member. But, in a way, it is. If the Hall is viewed as only for the most elite athletes, Gatti doesn't stand a chance. He wasn't a great fighter, but his flaws made him even more appealing.

The word that comes to mind is *entertaining*. An athlete who entertains is often remembered more fondly than a more talented adversary. Gatti was never boring. He always gave everything he had and left pieces of himself in various boxing arenas on the East Coast.

There have been other athletes in sport whose ability to enthrall us eclipsed their talent.

Former New York Jets quarterback Joe Namath is not remembered for the numerous interceptions he threw. His career stats are rather on the average side, but Namath was dramatic and flashy. The single most important thing he did was predict his team's victory over the "unbeatable" Baltimore Colts in the 1969 Super Bowl. Namath guaranteed his Jets would win. Pundits and fans laughed. The Jets won the game, 16–7.

In 1960, Bill Mazeroski, second baseman for the Pittsburgh Pirates, hit one of the most memorable home runs in baseball history. It didn't matter that Mazeroski was a career .260 hitter. What did matter was that his home run in Game 7 of the World Series against the New York Yankees won the game, and the series.

Mazeroski, also arguably the best defensive second baseman of his era, was elected into the Baseball Hall of Fame in 2001. Namath joined the football elite in 1985.

The argument against Gatti hanging out with some of the best fighters in history is that he was good, but never great. His make-or-break style, plus an affinity for fighting aggressively when it wasn't necessary, made him vulnerable but also appealed to his fans.

Gatti was beaten by Angel Manfredy, whose name will never be added to a Hall of Fame ballot, and Ivan Robinson, not once, but twice. He also tasted defeat at the hands of Carlos Baldomir, Micky Ward, and Alfonso Gomez. Gatti was brutally stopped by Hall of Famer Oscar De La Hoya and toyed with by future Hall member Floyd Mayweather Jr. The difference in talent in those fights was palpable.

But Gatti does have some impressive wins on his record. He beat Tracy Harris Patterson twice, knocked out Gabriel Ruelas in a classic slugfest, defeated Micky Ward twice, and, in the last meaningful win of his career, stopped former champion Jesse James Leija. The Ward victories cemented his legacy. Gatti got up from a brutal body shot when many at ringside, including esteemed trainer Emanuel Steward, didn't think it was possible. A year later, during his third fight with Ward, he broke his hand but refused to quit.

Gatti racked up a career-record 40 victories in 49 fights, with 31 knockouts. There are a number of fighters in the Hall with more career losses. This suggests that a boxer's record is only part of what the voters are looking at.

A fighter in Gatti's class, when considering heart and determination, was former light heavyweight champion Matthew Saad Muhammad. He was Gatti, plus 30 pounds. Saad Muhammad captured the light heavyweight belt in 1979, but after being stopped twice by Dwight Muhammad Qawi three years later, he was never the same fighter. His record shows 16 losses, many of them tallied after losing his title. Yet, in 1998, Saad Muhammad was elected to the Boxing Hall of Fame.

Gatti has plenty of ammunition to bolster his case for induction.

He participated in a "Fight of the Year" four times in seven years. He was never boring, almost always compelling, and virtually impossible to root against. His fights were full of endless drama. Gatti was a real-life "Rocky," coming from behind routinely to snatch victory from defeat. He was a throwback, a hardscrabble tough guy, a man who could define "party animal." He had become an icon by the time his career ended, one of the most popular fighters of his era. His longevity might have been the most impressive part of his resume. For a guy who was rarely in an easy fight, his peak years were from 1995 to 2005. That's 10 years of hell.

Gatti's premature death likely helped him with some voters. Sentimentality can be a powerful proponent. Did Gatti deserve to be elected into the International Boxing Hall of Fame? The answer is yes.

Talent isn't always the most important factor, as Gatti proved again and again. His ability to astound, with resiliency, and a heart that seemed twice the size of his 140-pound frame was enough for the Hall voters to welcome him with open arms.

You did good, "Thunder."

# APPENDIX A

## Memories of Gatti, Ward, and the Trilogy

"**F**rom ringside in Atlantic City in 1997, I saw all but the last shred of sense leave Gatti's body when Gabriel Ruelas caught him with an uppercut. Gatti's face, whipped around in my direction by the blow, was screwed up into a tight little bunch of features, eyes squeezed shut and mouth pursed clumsily around the bulk of the mouthpiece. He lurched across the ring, pursued by Ruelas, who hit him with abandon but could not put him down. Gatti somehow recovered and fought back; I saw his body come back to life as full consciousness reentered it. In the next round he poleaxed Ruelas with a left hook, the same punch with which Gatti knocked out Wilson Rodriguez in 1996, after Rodriguez had pounded both of Gatti's eyes nearly closed and staggered and floored him with punches he couldn't see coming."—Carlo Rotella, director of American Studies at Boston College, writing in *New York Times Magazine*, December 2009[1]

"I saw tears rolling down his eyes. He said, 'My side hurts, but I'm going to make it through the last round.' I told him I wasn't going to let him get hurt, that if I didn't see some bounce, I was going to stop the fight. He got up and started bouncing in the corner. He finished the fight."—Buddy McGirt, Gatti's trainer, July 2006, recalling round 1 of Gatti–Ward I[2]

"People love to see warriors go to war. This is the television business. At the end of the day, we're about entertainment. [Gatti] entertains you with his style, with his fists."—Kery Davis, senior vice president for programming at HBO Sports[3]

"Arturo bought a BMW before [the Wilson Rodriguez] fight, and I told him not to. After the fight, he said to me, 'Two things went through my mind when I was on the ground. No. 1, Pat Lynch is having a heart attack. No. 2, there goes my BMW.'"—Pat Lynch, Gatti's manager[4]

"Smash him with a right hand that splits an eyebrow, causing blood to pour down his face. Crush him with a body shot that caves in a rib. Pound him until his legs become too shaky to support his body. Arturo Gatti will accept all that stoically, without malice. He always has, knowing it's part of boxing, the cruel and, for Gatti, often painful sport in which he makes a living. Just don't ignore him, dismiss him, or show him a lack of respect. That, he can't accept."—Steve Springer, *Los Angeles Times*, March 2001[5]

"When Ivan Robinson and Arturo Gatti met at center ring to start the 10th and final round Saturday night at the Trump Taj Mahal, they touched gloves and looked deeply into each other's eyes. Then they dropped their heads forward so their foreheads gently touched.

"It was a moving tribute, a caress, a touch of class by two warriors who had fought tooth and toenail for the second time in four months.

"For Robinson, who had narrowly outpointed the reckless, brawling Gatti in their August bout, it was an exceptional gesture, for this time he had endured a disgraceful number of low blows from the desperate Canadian. This time, he won by a larger margin."—Jay Searcy, *Philadelphia Inquirer*, December 1998[6]

"It is the longest night. I always have trouble sleeping. You see everything chasing you—in your mind, in your dreams. You see burgers and sodas chasing you, because you want it and you know you can't have it. It's so close to the weigh-in, you start thinking about food because you know the next day, after the weigh-in, you can eat anything."—Arturo Gatti, January 1998[7]

"Gatti has made millions and taken enough punishment for several life-times. Still, it will be hard for fans to let him go. Last summer, Mike Tyson took his final beating, at age 39, and decided it was time to bow out. But Tyson never staged a comeback in the ring. Every time he was losing, he quit. Gatti has made a career out of resurgence."—Don Steinberg, *Philadelphia Inquirer*, July 2006, after Gatti lost to Carlos Baldomir[8]

"You can't give a fighter higher accolades than to say he always gave fans more than their money's worth."—J. Russell Peltz, who held a 40 percent promotional share of Gatti[9]

"Maybe I could fight a little more cautiously, but that wouldn't be me. I've come to accept that."—Arturo Gatti, after losing to Angel Manfredy[10]

"Hasta la vista, baby. I did my best, I came in thinking I could outbox him, but the ring kept getting smaller and smaller. I can't keep taking this abuse no more."—Arturo Gatti, after losing his final fight to Alfonso Gomez[11]

"Over a period of 13 months they spent a total of 90 minutes beating the shit out of each other, drawing blood, raising welts, puncturing eardrums, abusing livers (above and beyond what Gatti did during a typical night on the town), breaking hands, and knocking each other to the canvas—and each time when it was over, they fell into an embrace. First they bowed their heads and brought their foreheads together, then Ward draped his gloves around Gatti's neck, then Gatti did the same, then assorted managers and matchmakers closed in to take part, then Arturo and Micky spoke a few words to each other, then they separated for a second, and finally they came in close for a tight, traditional, chin-on-the-other-guy's-shoulder hug. Boxers almost always come to respect the hell out of each other by the end of a hard fight. But this was something different."—Eric Raskin, Grantland.com, after Ward–Gatti III[12]

"The face Gatti wears while kneeling by the referee's count certainly doesn't suggest he will rise again. That he does and even almost wins the fight go beyond telling us everything we ever need to know about Gatti to almost beginning to tell us what we need to know about ourselves, and I am not going to explain that further beyond asking you to look at that face again."—Sergio De La Pava, on Gatti's reaction to the body shot Micky Ward delivered in round 9 of their first fight in 2002 [13]

"[Gatti] was the greatest fan-friendly TV fighter I've ever been associated with. I called him the 'Human Highlight Film.' He lived with an over-abundance of passion. He fought hard, he lived hard, he played hard, and he partied hard. He raced through life."—Lou Duva, Gatti's manager [14]

"I used to wonder what would happen if I fought my twin. Now I know."—Arturo Gatti, after his first fight with Micky Ward [15]

"While I'm shouting, 'You can stop it anytime, [referee] Frank [Cappuccino], stop the fight,' there's part of me inside that's saying: 'Stop that. This isn't professional.' You know, I was literally out of control because the fight was out of control, the crowd was out of control, the moment was out of control."—Jim Lampley, *HBO World Championship Boxing*, on calling the action for HBO during round 9 of Gatti–Ward I [16]

"The two of them together created history. Neither one could have done it by himself. But together, they became iconic."—Kathy Duva, Gatti's promoter [17]

"It ended as it had to, with a short, sad, left hook to the body. That's the way Micky Ward went out with his old friend and great nemesis Arturo Gatti when he said his last good-bye four and a half years ago. It was a left hook to Gatti's coffin."—Ron Borges, *Boston Herald*, October 2013 [18]

"[Gatti] was North Jersey. He came from another country, but he was one of us and they knew it. When he got hit, they got hit. When he bled, they bled. And when he won, they won. He was their kind of guy. Before the Mayweather fight, we had to do a studio shot with HBO, so Pat [Lynch, the manager] and Buddy [McGirt, the trainer] and Ted Cruz [the conditioner] and I are standing in front of his apartment house and this limo about the size of a battleship pulls up and he says, 'What's that?' Pat says, 'It's for us,' and Arturo says, 'Not anymore.' Arturo walks over to the driver and hands him 200 bucks and tells him, 'This isn't us. Take the day off.'

"Then he gets in his car and we get in and he drives, no retinue, nobody to hold the door and patronize him, just friends like always. We get to the tunnel and the [Port Authority] cops and toll-takers all recognize us and they are shouting, 'Hey, Arturo, you gonna beat that guy?' To them he wasn't a star. He was more than that. He was Arturo from the block."—Carl Moretti, New Jersey matchmaker[19]

"I wasn't a wise guy. I even tried night school later on, but it wasn't for me. My father made me go to work for him as an electrician. I wasn't very good. Hey, I was terrible. If it weren't for boxing, I could have been responsible for burning down half of Montreal."—Arturo Gatti, on his youth[20]

"Even when Arturo Gatti was the main-eventer, he still fought with the passion of a club fighter . . . the honest workman who never checked his hunger at the door just because life was easy and he had a world title. He fought a puncher named Micky Ward three times in matches so brutal and so passionate that they could have fought inside a pay telephone booth."—Jerry Izenberg, *New Jersey Star-Ledger*, July 2009[21]

"They are remembered not for Gatti winning two to Ward's one but, as heroes, because they kept agreeing to fight each other for the pride, for the entertainment of the crowds . . . and for the hell of it."—Jeff Powell, *Daily Mail*, January 2011[22]

"He will forever be a guy I will use when motivating my fighters in times of duress. Like Pazienza, Holyfield, and Hagler before him, I will find myself telling a fighter between rounds, Arturo Gatti went through all that he went through all those times, but you can't even find it in yourself to suck it up for another three rounds of a tough fight?"—"Iceman" John Scully, boxing trainer[23]

"It feels good knowing I contributed to him hopefully getting in, but you know, he had a lot of great fights other than our three fights. I like to consider it the icing on the cake, if you want to call it that. He has had some of the best fights, best rounds in boxing for that matter, so it should stick cause he deserves it, he was a blood and guts warrior, so I think he deserves it."—Micky Ward, on the role the trilogy played in Gatti's induction into the International Boxing Hall of Fame[24]

"What mattered more than whether Gatti won or lost . . . is that you knew you were going to get a show. Every. Time. Gatti was as tough, nearly, as humans get. Nobody fought through more blood streaming down his face, through more swollen eyes, through more broken hands. Nobody took the kind of punishment Gatti took in fights and was as much of a threat to come back and win by knockout. Gatti was in four *Ring* magazine Fights of the Year, and he was in plenty of other contenders for that title."—Tim Starks, *Queensberry Rules*, July 2009[25]

"He just never gave up. And he knew at any given time, he could knock you out. And he knew that he could kill you. Basically that's what he did. He senses [*sic*], he seeked, and he destroyed. He was like a missile. Once that missile had its target, it got you and it exploded. And that's just what Arturo Gatti was."—Ivan Robinson, two-time Gatti opponent[26]

"[Gatti] was the greatest action fighter of our era, and maybe one of the top two or three action fighters of all time."—Dan Rafael, *ESPN Sports*[27]

"I never saw a crowd show so much love for someone like the way that the crowds flocked to Arturo's fights in Atlantic City. I mean, they were so into him, and the crowds were electric. He just fought his heart out every fight."—Randy Neumann, referee[28]

"You can't train for it—either you have it or you don't. You're born with it, I think. It's not something like strength or speed. Something like that, your will, you're either born with it or you're not. Everybody's heart is the same size. It's your will to be able to take punches or go through pain and not give up."—Micky Ward, on heart and will[29]

"How Micky lasted, that's a testimony to his inner self, because he doesn't quit. He'd have fought that kid until tomorrow. If that kid didn't knock Micky out, that fight is still going on."—Mickey O'Keefe, neighborhood friend and boxing coach, on Micky Ward's determination to survive to the final bell in his fight against Mike Mungin, who out-weighed him by 20 pounds[30]

"I thought [the movie] was good. It was pretty true. Obviously it's hard to tell two people's lives in two hours, but they did a very good job. They made things a little more dramatic, but it was pretty much on. Mark Wahlberg, Christian Bale, Amy Adams, Melissa Leo, they all did a great job.

"So many women have come up to me and said they loved the movie because it pertained to women and men. Women loved it because of the crazy sisters, the dominating mother. That's real, and I think they took to that.

"[My sisters] didn't say nice things right after. At first they were a little mad. They were a little upset about the way they were portrayed. I said, 'You're lucky they really didn't portray you the right way. If they had it would have been really worse.'"—Micky Ward, on *The Fighter*[31]

"If someone had told me 10 years ago when I lost all those fights and retired from boxing that someday I'd make a million bucks from one fight, I'd have thought they were crazy."—Micky Ward, after earning $1.2 million for his third fight against Arturo Gatti

"It's not about who's tougher. We're both tough guys. It's about respect. In the ring, we tried to kill each other. But I have a lot of respect for Arturo. I like him; he's a nice person. I'd never say anything bad about him, and I think that he feels the same way about me. I wanted to beat him more than anything in the world. But outside the ring, he's a beauti-ful guy."—Micky Ward, on his relationship with Gatti

"Arturo's death really shook me up. It was a terrible tragedy. I wasn't there, so I can't tell you what happened. But it's hard for me to believe that he killed himself."—Micky Ward

"There are fights in the film that bear no relationship to what actually happened. And the make-believe world championship fight at the end is ridiculous. Micky never won a world title. When he beat Shea Neary in London [the climactic scene in *The Fighter*], it was for a belt given out by a silly alphabet-soup organization called the World Boxing Union. That belt meant so little to Micky that he gave it up rather than defend it. The great thing about Micky Ward is that he's appreciated and respected by people who know boxing even though he never won a world title. Why construct a nonsense story line and pretend that fiction is history?"—George Kimball, *Boston Herald* boxing writer, on *The Fighter*[32]

"I loved boxing. The one-on-one, the competition. Being a fighter is about sacrificing your body and doing everything you can within the rules to win. I gave boxing everything that was in me. I never cut corners in training or in a fight. I started my career at 140 pounds and I finished my career at 140 pounds, which tells you how hard I worked to stay in shape. I still follow boxing."—Micky Ward[33]

"Some people like a lot of attention. I don't. I'm happy being in the background, so the movie won't change my life. I'm just a regular guy, the same old me. Don't worry; I won't go Hollywood on you."—Micky Ward[34]

"He is the type of fighter whose legend will only grow larger as more times goes by. He was always a stand-up guy, whether it was in the ring as a boxer, in the streets where, if provoked, he could be a tremendous street fighter, or when dealing with his very large and dysfunctional family."—Adam Berlin, *Sweet Science*, December 2007, on Micky Ward[35]

"I'd say I knew him very well, and he was a great guy, and he loved you very much, and he was a Hall of Fame boxer, but, more than that, he was a Hall of Fame man."—Micky Ward, when asked what he'd tell Arturo Gatti's children about their father[36]

"The fact that he was a prideful Irish fighter, the kind of fighter—I'm sure it's true of other ethnicities, as well, but it does feel to me that a lot of the Irish guys are this way—who absolutely will not quit; Micky was like that."—Bob Halloran, author of the Micky Ward biography *Irish Thunder*[37]

"Micky told me a story that I'm not sure he's ever told anybody. In the sixth round of the second Gatti fight, Gatti hit him in the temple really hard, and it blinded him—he went back to his corner seeing nothing but didn't want anybody to know because he didn't want to stop fighting. So he sat there hearing voices, being rubbed down, hoping that it would come back. But the bell rang and he still couldn't see anything, but he knew Gatti would approach him, so he just waited. Gatti immediately nailed him in the temple again, and he got his sight back."—Louis C.K., comedian and friend of Micky Ward[38]

"Deep in their hearts, did it really matter who won the third fight, or was it more about honoring the way they were, and the way they did what they did. I think you could poll 100 devoted boxing fans who were avid watchers of that rivalry right now and ask them who won the three fights, and I'm guessing less than 40 percent would be able to tell you that Arturo won fights two and three, and Micky won number one. People don't remember that. They remember the sacrifice, the combat, the mayhem, and the love. That's really what this rivalry provided."—Jim Lampley, *HBO World Championship Boxing*[39]

"They emptied themselves for us. They gave up a piece of their lives for us. Um . . . thanks guys."—Larry Merchant, *HBO World Championship Boxing*[40]

To Gatti and Ward, the only title that means anything is 'warrior.' The only belts that mean anything are the ones they punch each other with. These are character actors who want starring roles—soldiers who want battlefield commissions."—Larry Merchant, *HBO World Championship Boxing*, before the 2002 Gatti–Ward bout[41]

# APPENDIX B

## Boxing Records

**K**ey to abbreviations: unanimous decision (UD), split decision (SD), majority decision (MD), retired technical decision (RTD), technical decision (TD), knockout (KO), technical knockout (TKO), points (PTS).

### MICKY WARD (LOWELL, MASSACHUSETTS). CAREER RECORD: 38–13, 27 KNOCKOUTS.

| Date | Opponent | Opponent's Record (W–L–D) | Location | Result/ Round |
|------|----------|---------------------------|----------|---------------|
| 2003-06-07 | Arturo Gatti | 35–6–0 | Boardwalk Hall, Atlantic City, New Jersey, USA | L UD/10 |
| 2002-11-23 | Arturo Gatti | 34–6–0 | Boardwalk Hall, Atlantic City, New Jersey, USA | L UD/10 |
| 2002-05-18 | Arturo Gatti | 34–5–0 | Mohegan Sun Casino, Uncasville, Connecticut, USA | W MD/10 |
| 2002-01-05 | Jesse James Leija | 42–5–2 | Freeman Coliseum, San Antonio, Texas, USA | L TD/5 |
| 2001-07-13 | Emanuel Augustus | 24–17–4 | Hampton Beach Casino, Hampton Beach, New Hampshire, USA | W UD/10 |
| 2001-05-18 | Steve Quinonez | 25–5–1 | Foxwoods Resort, Mashantucket, Connecticut, USA | W KO/1 |

| | | | | |
|---|---|---|---|---|
| 2000-08-19 | Antonio Diaz | 34–2–0 | Foxwoods Resort, Mashantucket, Connecticut, USA | L UD/10 |
| 2000-03-11 | Shea Neary[a] | 22–0–0 | Olympia, Kensington, London, United Kingdom | W TKO/8 |
| 1999-10-01 | Reggie Green | 30–3–0 | Icenter, Salem, New Hampshire, USA | W TKO/10 |
| 1999-07-16 | Jermal Corbin | 17–2–0 | Hampton Beach Casino, Hampton Beach, New Hampshire, USA | W RTD/5 |
| 1999-03-17 | Jose Luis Mendez | 3–11–1 | Roxy, Boston, Massachusetts, USA | W TKO/3 |
| 1998-06-07 | Zab Judah[b] | 15–0–0 | Miccosukee Indian Gaming Resort, Miami, Florida, USA | L UD/12 |
| 1998-04-14 | Mark Fernandez | 33–17–1 | Foxwoods Resort, Mashantucket, Connecticut, USA | W KO/3 |
| 1997-08-09 | Vince Phillips[c] | 36–3–0 | Roxy, Boston, Massachusetts, USA | L TKO/3 |
| 1997-04-12 | Alfonso "Poncho" Sanchez | 16–0–0 | Thomas & Mack Center, Las Vegas, Nevada, USA | W KO/7 |
| 1996-12-06 | Manny Castillo | 13–6–2 | Lawlor Events Center, Reno, Nevada, USA | W SD/10 |
| 1996-07-28 | Louis "The Viper" Veader | 31–1–0 | Foxwoods Resort, Mashantucket, Connecticut, USA | W UD/12 |
| 1996-04-13 | Louis "The Viper" Veader | 31–0–0 | Fleet Center, Boston, Massachusetts, USA | W TKO/9 |
| 1996-03-15 | Alex Ortiz | 0–5–0 | Wonderland Ballroom, Revere, Massachusetts, USA | W TKO/1 |
| 1996-01-26 | Alberto Alicea | 6–31–0 | Wonderland Ballroom, Revere, Massachusetts, USA | W TKO/3 |
| 1995-12-30 | Edgardo Rosario | | Wonderland Greyhound Park, Revere, Massachusetts, USA | W TKO/1 |
| 1994-09-10 | Genaro Andujar | 8–10–1 | Lowell Auditorium, Lowell, Massachusetts, USA | W KO/3 |
| 1994-06-17 | Luis Castillo | 5–10–0 | Sheraton Inn, Lowell, Massachusetts, USA | W TKO/5 |
| 1991-10-15 | Ricky Meyers | 15–1–0 | Harrah's Trump Plaza Hotel, Atlantic City, New Jersey, USA | L UD/10 |
| 1991-05-02 | Tony Martin | 22–3–0 | Trump Taj Mahal, Atlantic City, New Jersey, USA | L UD/10 |
| 1990-10-18 | Charles Murray[d] | 17-0-0 | War Memorial Auditorium, Rochester, New York, USA | L UD/12 |
| 1990-04-26 | Harold Brazier[e] | 67–10–1 | Resorts International, Atlantic City, New Jersey, USA | L UD/12 |

| | | | | |
|---|---|---|---|---|
| 1990-02-03 | David Rivello | 14–1–0 | Hynes Convention Center, Boston, Massachusetts, USA | W SD/10 |
| 1989-05-23 | Clarence Coleman | 13–3–1 | Showboat Hotel & Casino, Atlantic City, New Jersey, USA | W TKO/5 |
| 1989-01-15 | Frankie "Panchito" Warren[f] | 28–1–0 | Caesars Hotel & Casino, Atlantic City, New Jersey, USA | L UD/12 |
| 1988-12-13 | Francisco Tomas da Cruz | 30–3–0 | Resorts International, Atlantic City, New Jersey, USA | W TKO/3 |
| 1988-09-09 | Mike Mungin | 17–2–0 | Resorts International, Atlantic City, New Jersey, USA | L UD/10 |
| 1988-07-09 | Marvin Garris | 14–8–1 | Sands Casino Hotel, Atlantic City, New Jersey, USA | W TKO/2 |
| 1988-05-19 | David Silva | 1–7–0 | Resorts International, Atlantic City, New Jersey, USA | W UD/10 |
| 1988-02-19 | Joey Olivera | 20–12–1 | Bally's Las Vegas, Las Vegas, Nevada, USA | W UD/10 |
| 1988-01-15 | Joey Ferrell | 7–7–2 | Resorts International, Atlantic City, New Jersey, USA | W TKO/1 |
| 1987-09-25 | Edwin Curet | 21–7–2 | Resorts Hotel & Casino, Atlantic City, New Jersey, USA | L SD/10 |
| 1987-08-25 | Derrick McGuire | 13–4–0 | Bally's Park Place Hotel Casino, Atlantic City, New Jersey, USA | W TKO/4 |
| 1987-04-06 | Kelly Koble | 12–5–1 | Caesars Palace, Outdoor Arena, Las Vegas, Nevada, USA | W TKO/4 |
| 1987-02-24 | Hilario Mercedes | 4–4–0 | Resorts International, Atlantic City, New Jersey, USA | W SD/8 |
| 1986-10-24 | Carlos Brandi | | Lowell Auditorium, Lowell, Massachusetts, USA | W KO/2 |
| 1986-08-29 | John Rafuse | 12–2–0 | Lowell Auditorium, Lowell, Massachusetts, USA | W UD/8 |
| 1986-07-04 | Rafael Terrero | 1–4–0 | Resorts International, Atlantic City, New Jersey, USA | W TKO/2 |
| 1986-06-15 | Ken Willis | 5–14–6 | Trump Casino Hotel, Atlantic City, New Jersey, USA | W PTS/6 |
| 1986-05-30 | Luis Pizarro | 1–1–0 | Trump Casino Hotel, Atlantic City, New Jersey, USA | W TKO/3 |
| 1986-04-18 | Darrell Curtis | 6–3–1 | Trump Casino Hotel, Atlantic City, New Jersey, USA | W TKO/5 |
| 1986-02-21 | Jesus Carlos Velez | 0–6–0 | Trump Casino Hotel, Atlantic City, New Jersey, USA | W KO/6 |
| 1986-01-24 | Mike Peoples | 4–10–3 | Resorts International, Atlantic City, New Jersey, USA | W UD/4 |

| 1986-01-10 | Chris Bajor | 4–3–3 | Resorts International, Atlantic City, New Jersey, USA | W TKO/3 |
| 1985-08-27 | Greg Young | 1–2–0 | Memorial Auditorium, Lowell, Massachusetts, USA | W TKO/4 |
| 1985-06-13 | David Morin | 4–3–0 | Roll on America Skating Rink, Lawrence, Massachusetts, USA | W TKO/1 |

[a] WBU (original 1995–2004) super lightweight title
[b] Interim USBA super lightweight title
[c] IBF World super lightweight title
[d] USBA super lightweight title
[e] IBF Intercontinental super lightweight title
[f] USBA super lightweight title

## ARTURO GATTI (JERSEY CITY, NEW JERSEY). CAREER RECORD: 40–9, 31 KNOCKOUTS.

| Date | Opponent | Opponent's Record (W–L–D) | Location | Result/ Round |
| --- | --- | --- | --- | --- |
| 2007-07-14 | Alfonso Gomez | 16–3–2 | Boardwalk Hall, Atlantic City, New Jersey, USA | L TKO/7 |
| 2006-07-22 | Carlos Baldomir[a] | 42–9–6 | Boardwalk Hall, Atlantic City, New Jersey, USA | L TKO/9 |
| 2006-01-28 | Thomas Damgaard[b] | 37–0–0 | Boardwalk Hall, Atlantic City, New Jersey, USA | W TKO/11 |
| 2005-06-25 | Floyd Mayweather Jr[c] | 33–0–0 | Boardwalk Hall, Atlantic City, New Jersey, USA | L RTD/6 |
| 2005-01-29 | Jesse James Leija[c] | 47–6–2 | Boardwalk Hall, Atlantic City, New Jersey, USA | W KO/5 |
| 2004-07-24 | Leonard Dorin[c] | 22–0–1 | Boardwalk Hall, Atlantic City, New Jersey, USA | W KO/2 |
| 2004-01-24 | Gianluca Branco[d] | 32–0–1 | Boardwalk Hall, Atlantic City, New Jersey, USA | W UD/12 |
| 2003-06-07 | Micky Ward | 38–12–0 | Boardwalk Hall, Atlantic City, New Jersey, USA | W UD/10 |
| 2002-11-23 | Micky Ward | 38–11–0 | Boardwalk Hall, Atlantic City, New Jersey, USA | W UD/10 |
| 2002-05-18 | Micky Ward | 37–11–0 | Mohegan Sun Casino, Uncasville, Connecticut, USA | L MD/10 |

| | | | | |
|---|---|---|---|---|
| 2002-01-26 | Terron Millett | 26–2–1 | Madison Square Garden Theater, New York, New York, USA | W TKO/4 |
| 2001-03-24 | Oscar De La Hoya | 32–2–0 | MGM Grand, Las Vegas, Nevada, USA | L TKO/5 |
| 2000-09-08 | Joe Hutchinson | 18–0–2 | Molson Centre, Montreal, Quebec, Canada | W UD/10 |
| 2000-04-29 | Eric Jakubowski | 20–6–0 | Madison Square Garden, New York, New York, USA | W TKO/2 |
| 2000-02-26 | Joey Gamache | 55–3–0 | Madison Square Garden, New York, New York, USA | W KO/2 |
| 1999-08-14 | Reyes Munoz | 21–3–0 | Foxwoods Resort, Mashantucket, Connecticut, USA | W TKO/1 |
| 1998-12-12 | Ivan Robinson | 26–2–0 | Trump Taj Mahal, Atlantic City, New Jersey, USA | L UD/10 |
| 1998-08-22 | Ivan Robinson | 25–2–0 | Convention Hall, Atlantic City, New Jersey, USA | L SD/10 |
| 1998-01-17 | Angel Manfredy | 22–2–1 | Convention Hall, Atlantic City, New Jersey, USA | L TKO/8 |
| 1997-10-04 | Gabriel Ruelas[e] | 44–3–0 | Caesars Hotel & Casino, Atlantic City, New Jersey, USA | W TKO/5 |
| 1997-05-04 | Calvin Grove | 49–8–0 | Caesars Hotel & Casino, Atlantic City, New Jersey, USA | W RTD/7 |
| 1997-02-22 | Tracy Harris Patterson[e] | 57–4–1 | Convention Center, Atlantic City, New Jersey, USA | W UD/12 |
| 1996-07-11 | Feliciano Correa | 15–5–0 | Madison Square Garden, New York, New York, USA | W KO/3 |
| 1996-03-23 | Wilson Rodriguez[e] | 44–8–3 | Madison Square Garden Theater, New York, New York, USA | W KO/6 |
| 1995-12-15 | Tracy Harris Patterson[e] | 54–3–1 | Madison Square Garden, New York, New York, USA | W UD/12 |
| 1995-10-07 | Carlos Vergara | 16–11–0 | Convention Center, Atlantic City, New Jersey, USA | W TKO/1 |
| 1995-07-13 | Barrington Francis | 21–6–4 | Caesars Hotel & Casino, Atlantic City, New Jersey, USA | W TKO/6 |
| 1995-04-22 | Tialano Tovar | 9–8–1 | Bally's Park Place Hotel Casino, Atlantic City, New Jersey, USA | W KO/1 |
| 1995-03-09 | Ruslan Smolenkov | 0–3–0 | Martinihal, Groningen, Netherlands | W KO/1 |
| 1994-11-22 | Jose Sanabria[f] | 21–10–3 | Meadowlands Convention Center, Secaucus, New Jersey, USA | W UD/12 |
| 1994-08-16 | Richard Salazar[f] | 13–5–2 | Blue Horizon, Philadelphia, Pennsylvania, USA | W TKO/10 |

| | | | | |
|---|---|---|---|---|
| 1994-06-28 | Pete Taliaferro[f] | 25–2–0 | Meadowlands Convention Center, Secaucus, New Jersey, USA | W TKO/1 |
| 1994-05-06 | Darrell Singleton | 9–3–1 | Boardwalk Convention Center, Atlantic City, New Jersey, USA | W TKO/1 |
| 1994-01-08 | Leon Bostic | 12–3–1 | Friar Tuck Inn, Catskill, New York, USA | W MD/8 |
| 1993-11-11 | Glenn Irizarry | 3–7–0 | Huntington Hilton Hotel, Melville, New York, USA | W TKO/1 |
| 1993-10-23 | Derek Francis | 7–2–0 | Sands Casino Hotel, Atlantic City, New Jersey, USA | W KO/1 |
| 1993-08-24 | Luis Guzman | 0–2–0 | Merv Griffin's Resorts, Atlantic City, New Jersey, USA | W KO/1 |
| 1993-07-30 | Robert Scott | 1–2–0 | Ramada Hotel, New York, New York, USA | W KO/1 |
| 1993-06-20 | Christino Suero | 1–5–0 | Harrah's Marina Hotel Casino, Atlantic City, New Jersey, USA | W KO/3 |
| 1993-05-15 | Clifford Hicks | 13–11–0 | Memorial High School Gym, Brick Town, New Jersey, USA | W KO/3 |
| 1993-04-07 | Curtis Mathis | 3–11–1 | Newark, New Jersey, USA | W TKO/3 |
| 1993-03-23 | Plamen Gechev | 4–5–0 | Sportpaleis Ahoy', Rotterdam, Netherlands | W TKO/1 |
| 1992-11-17 | King Solomon | 5–1–3 | Blue Horizon, Philadelphia, Pennsylvania, USA | L SD/6 |
| 1992-05-15 | Joe Lafontant | 2–2–1 | Trump Taj Mahal, Atlantic City, New Jersey, USA | W UD/6 |
| 1992-04-22 | Antonio Gonzalez | 1–5–0 | Meadowlands Arena, East Rutherford, New Jersey, USA | W TKO/1 |
| 1991-10-22 | Francisco Aguiano | | Blue Horizon, Philadelphia, Pennsylvania, USA | W TKO/1 |
| 1991-08-02 | Richard De Jesus | 1–0–0 | Quality Inn Hotel, Newark, New Jersey, USA | W TKO/1 |
| 1991-07-09 | Luis Melendez | 1–1–0 | Blue Horizon, Philadelphia, Pennsylvania, USA | W KO/1 |

| 1991-06-10 | Jose Gonzales | 0–1–0 | Meadowlands Convention Center, Secaucus, New Jersey, USA | W TKO/3 |

[a] WBC World welterweight title, IBA welterweight title
[b] Vacant IBA welterweight title
[c] WBC World super lightweight title
[d] Vacant WBC World super lightweight title
[e] IBF World super featherweight title
[f] USBA super featherweight title

## LARRY CARNEY (LOWELL, MASSACHUSETTS). CAREER RECORD: 28–11–2, 19 KNOCKOUTS.

| Date | Opponent | Opponent's Record (W–L–D) | Location | Result/ Round |
|------|----------|---------------------------|----------|---------------|
| 1971-05-17 | Tony Licata | 20–0–1 | Curtis Hixon Hall, Tampa, Florida, USA | L TKO/4 |
| 1971-02-18 | Georgie Johnson | 54–18–0 | Portland, Maine, USA | L TKO/7 |
| 1970-12-15 | Bobby Covino | 14–0–1 | Boston Garden, Boston, Massachusetts, USA | L UD/10 |
| 1970-09-28 | Jose Cole | | Providence, Rhode Island, USA | W KO/2 |
| 1970-09-25 | Bob Simmons | 12–18–4 | Arena, Boston, Massachusetts, USA | W SD/8 |
| 1970-09-03 | Bob Benoit | 25–4–0 | Exposition Building, Portland, Maine, USA | L UD/10 |
| 1970-07-27 | Tony Fernandez | 1–4–0 | Arena, Boston, Massachusetts, USA | W UD/8 |
| 1969-01-14 | Gomeo Brennan | 76–19–6 | Auditorium, Miami Beach, Florida, USA | L TKO/5 |
| 1968-12-05 | Gene Roberts | 4–2–0 | Roseland Ballroom, Taunton, Massachusetts, USA | W TKO/6 |
| 1967-12-21 | Jimmy McDermott[a] | 33–9–3 | Exposition Building, Portland, Maine, USA | L TKO/1 |
| 1967-08-31 | Bobby Warthen | 11–9–0 | Exposition Building, Portland, Maine, USA | L TKO/7 |
| 1967-07-13 | Pete Riccitelli[a] | 32–6–1 | Exposition Building, Portland, Maine, USA | W UD/12 |

| | | | | |
|---|---|---|---|---|
| 1967-06-15 | Joe Brown | 0–4–0 | Exposition Building, Portland, Maine, USA | W TKO/5 |
| 1965-03-26 | Eddie Owens | 13–2–1 | Mechanics Hall, Worcester, Massachusetts, USA | W TKO/5 |
| 1964-12-14 | Joe DeNucci | 37–10–3 | Boston Garden, Boston, Massachusetts, USA | W PTS/10 |
| 1964-09-18 | Leonard Eani | | Burlington, Vermont, USA | W KO/2 |
| 1964-03-16 | Mick Leahy | 44–14–7 | Boston Garden, Boston, Massachusetts, USA | L UD/10 |
| 1964-02-17 | Joe DeNucci | 36–6–3 | Boston Garden, Boston, Massachusetts, USA | W SD/10 |
| 1963-12-09 | Joe DeNucci | 36–6–2 | Boston Garden, Boston, Massachusetts, USA | W PTS/10 |
| 1963-10-04 | Augie Simmons | 1–11–1 | Arena, Boston, Massachusetts, USA | W TKO/2 |
| 1963-09-16 | Felix Santiago | 9–14–4 | Arena, Boston, Massachusetts, USA | W KO/7 |
| 1963-08-12 | Frankie Olivera | 10–13–4 | Sargent Field, New Bedford, Massachusetts, USA | L UD/10 |
| 1963-07-15 | Vernon LaMar | 3–9–1 | Sargent Field, New Bedford, Massachusetts, USA | W TKO/8 |
| 1963-06-10 | Gaylord Barnes | 6–24–0 | Arena, Boston, Massachusetts, USA | W PTS/10 |
| 1963-03-28 | Joe Gomes | 15–9–0 | Mechanics Hall, Worcester, Massachusetts, USA | L TKO/4 |
| 1963-03-18 | Willie Greene[b] | 30–6–0 | Boston Garden, Boston, Massachusetts, USA | W TKO/7 |
| 1963-03-07 | Vernon LaMar | 3–8–1 | Mechanics Hall, Worcester, Massachusetts, USA | W PTS/8 |
| 1963-02-28 | Hank Jones | 0–11–0 | Mechanics Hall, Worcester, Massachusetts, USA | W KO/1 |
| 1963-02-21 | Tom Tucker | 0–1–0 | Mechanics Hall, Worcester, Massachusetts, USA | W PTS/8 |
| 1963-02-07 | Peachy Davis[c] | 10–2–0 | Boston Garden, Boston, Massachusetts, USA | W TKO/2 |
| 1963-01-03 | Vernon LaMar | 3–7–1 | Mechanics Hall, Worcester, Massachusetts, USA | W UD/8 |
| 1962-12-20 | Augie Simmons | 0–4–0 | Mechanics Hall, Worcester, Massachusetts, USA | W UD/6 |
| 1962-05-11 | Freeman Turner | 0–1–0 | Mechanics Hall, Worcester, Massachusetts, USA | W TKO/4 |

| 1962-04-07 | Freeman Turner | | Boston Garden, Boston, Massachusetts, USA | W TKO/3 |
| 1962-01-26 | Gene Tapia | 3–3–0 | Mechanics Hall, Worcester, Massachusetts, USA | L TKO/8 |
| 1962-01-19 | Joe Arsenault | 4–0–0 | Mechanics Hall, Worcester, Massachusetts, USA | W TKO/2 |
| 1962-01-12 | Dobie Josie | 12–7–1 | Mechanics Hall, Worcester, Massachusetts, USA | W KO/2 |
| 1961-12-29 | Leroy Vincent | | Mechanics Hall, Worcester, Massachusetts, USA | W KO/1 |
| 1961-12-18 | Phil Wright | 1–2–0 | Providence, Rhode Island, USA | W KO/1 |
| 1961-12-15 | Don Webber | 9–7–2 | Mechanics Hall, Worcester, Massachusetts, USA | W TKO/2 |
| 1961-12-11 | Denny Goslow | 11–13–0 | Providence, Rhode Island, USA | W TKO/1 |

[a] USA New England light heavyweight title
[b] USA New England middleweight title
[c] Vacant USA New England middleweight title

## BEAU JAYNES (LOWELL, MASSACHUSETTS). CAREER RECORD: 52–45, 12 KNOCKOUTS.

| Date | Opponent | Opponent's Record (W–L–D) | Location | Result/ Round |
|------|----------|---------------------------|----------|---------------|
| 1979-05-11 | Mike Wyant | 16–3–0 | Cincinnati Gardens, Cincinnati, Ohio, USA | L KO/1 |
| 1979-04-14 | Rocky Fratto | 14–0–0 | War Memorial Auditorium, Syracuse, New York, USA | L TKO/7 |
| 1978-12-07 | Sean O'Grady | 60–1–0 | Oklahoma City, Oklahoma, USA | L TKO/2 |
| 1978-10-08 | Chris Clarke | 15–0–0 | Glace Bay Forum, Glace Bay, Nova Scotia, Canada | L TKO/5 |
| 1978-07-18 | Fernando Fernandez | 7–1–1 | Hynes Auditorium, Boston, Massachusetts, USA | L PTS/8 |
| 1978-03-24 | Alois Carmeliet | 24–4–1 | Zele, Oost-Vlaanderen, Belgium | L KO/3 |
| 1978-01-05 | Wilson Bell | 5–1–0 | Exposition Building, Portland, Maine, USA | L PTS/8 |

| 1977-12-16 | Fernando Fernandez | 5–0–1 | Lowell Auditorium, Lowell, Massachusetts, USA | L SD/8 |
|---|---|---|---|---|
| 1977-11-18 | Jose Papo Melendez | 4–10–0 | Lowell Auditorium, Lowell, Massachusetts, USA | W UD/8 |
| 1977-11-04 | Inocencio De la Rosa | 19–5–4 | Rif-stadion, Willemstad, Curaçao | L KO/5 |
| 1977-10-27 | Wilson Bell | 3–0–0 | Exposition Building, Portland, Maine, USA | W UD/8 |
| 1977-09-24 | Jimmy Corkum | 23–0–0 | Boston Garden, Boston, Massachusetts, USA | L PTS/10 |
| 1977-06-20 | Jimmy Corkum | 21–0–0 | Town Line Twin Rinks, Peabody, Massachusetts, USA | L KO/6 |
| 1977-04-22 | Jose Curet | 2–7–1 | JFK Memorial Coliseum, Manchester, New Hampshire, USA | W TKO/3 |
| 1976-12-21 | Tony Lopes[a] | 19–6–1 | Hynes Auditorium, Boston, Massachusetts, USA | L SD/10 |
| 1976-09-13 | Tony Lopes | 17–4–1 | Golden Banana Club, Peabody, Massachusetts, USA | W SD/10 |
| 1976-08-23 | Jim Henry | 11–21–3 | Golden Banana Club, Peabody, Massachusetts, USA | W SD/10 |
| 1976-07-17 | Antonio Cervantes | 75–10–3 | Maestranza Cesar Giron, Maracay, Venezuela | L KO/1 |
| 1976-05-13 | Tony Lopes[a] | 13–4–0 | Exposition Building, Portland, Maine, USA | L SD/10 |
| 1976-04-26 | Tony Lopes[a] | 11–4–0 | Boston Garden, Boston, Massachusetts, USA | L SD/10 |
| 1976-03-06 | Jo Kimpuani | 27–1–0 | Dunkirk, Nord, France | L KO/4 |
| 1975-12-20 | Tony Lopes[a] | 9–2–0 | Hynes Auditorium, Boston, Massachusetts, USA | W UD/10 |
| 1975-10-23 | Tony Lopes[a] | 7–1–0 | Exposition Building, Portland, Maine, USA | L SD/10 |
| 1975-09-30 | Joe DeFayette | 8–2–1 | Portland, Maine, USA | W SD/8 |
| 1975-04-06 | Lou Bizzarro | 16–0–0 | Erie, Pennsylvania, USA | L PTS/10 |
| 1975-02-08 | Clyde Gray | 45–3–1 | Toronto, Ontario, Canada | L TKO/7 |
| 1974-08-12 | Hector Matta | 23–7–2 | Coliseo Roberto Clemente, San Juan, Puerto Rico | L KO/4 |
| 1974-06-25 | Joe Carabella | 11–11–4 | Columbia Music Hall, West Hartford, Connecticut, USA | L PTS/8 |

| 1974-04-05 | Tony Petronelli[a] | 20–1–0 | WNAC-TV Studio, Boston, Massachusetts, USA | L UD/10 |
|---|---|---|---|---|
| 1974-02-28 | Jim Henry | 6–6–1 | Portland, Maine, USA | L PTS/10 |
| 1974-01-28 | Tony Petronelli | 19–1–0 | Boston University, Boston, Massachusetts, USA | L UD/10 |
| 1973-12-03 | Jose Resto | 5–34–2 | Colisee de Quebec, Quebec City, Quebec, Canada | W PTS/8 |
| 1973-11-22 | Don Sennett | 30–5–1 | Portland, Maine, USA | W UD/10 |
| 1973-11-01 | Jose Resto | 4–33–2 | Portland, Maine, USA | W PTS/8 |
| 1973-10-25 | Jose Resto | 4–32–2 | Exposition Building, Portland, Maine, USA | W PTS/8 |
| 1973-10-12 | Paul Poirier | 6–0–0 | Worcester, Massachusetts, USA | L SD/8 |
| 1973-09-10 | John Howard | 14–26–3 | Portland, Maine, USA | W TKO/6 |
| 1973-04-18 | Tony Petronelli | 11–1–0 | Brockton, Massachusetts, USA | L TKO/8 |
| 1973-04-06 | John Howard | 13–21–3 | Exposition Building, Portland, Maine, USA | L PTS/10 |
| 1972-12-01 | Pedro Carrasco | 105–3–2 | Madrid, Comunidad de Madrid, Spain | L TKO/6 |
| 1972-11-17 | Jose Pagan Rivera | 20–48–8 | Memorial Auditorium, Lowell, Massachusetts, USA | W UD/8 |
| 1972-10-12 | Rudy Bolds | 15–1–0 | Civic Arena, Pittsburgh, Pennsylvania, USA | L UD/10 |
| 1972-08-22 | Leo Randolph | 0–1–0 | IBEW Hall, Waltham, Massachusetts, USA | W KO/2 |
| 1972-07-24 | Don Sennett | 27–0–1 | IBEW Hall, Waltham, Massachusetts, USA | W SD/10 |
| 1972-06-27 | Richie Villanueva | 4–4–0 | Boston Garden, Boston, Massachusetts, USA | L TKO/3 |
| 1971-12-16 | Chuck Wilburn | 6–1–0 | Portland, Maine, USA | L TKO/7 |
| 1971-12-09 | Juan Ramos | 15–38–2 | Exposition Building, Portland, Maine, USA | W SD/10 |
| 1971-11-24 | Billy Wade | 2–8–0 | Arena, Waltham, Massachusetts, USA | W PTS/8 |
| 1971-10-14 | Chuck Wilburn | 2–1–0 | Portland, Maine, USA | L PTS/10 |

| 1971-08-26 | Bobby Richard | 23–8–0 | Exposition Building, Portland, Maine, USA | W UD/10 |
|---|---|---|---|---|
| 1971-04-29 | Sammy Goss | 21–2–0 | Arena, Philadelphia, Pennsylvania, USA | L KO/1 |
| 1971-03-16 | Frankie Otero | 29–1–1 | Auditorium, Miami Beach, Florida, USA | L UD/10 |
| 1971-01-07 | Bill Whittenburg | 8–8–2 | Exposition Building, Portland, Maine, USA | W UD/10 |
| 1970-12-15 | Castro Ramirez | 8–7–0 | Boston Garden, Boston, Massachusetts, USA | W TKO/10 |
| 1970-11-18 | Juan Ramos | 14–33–2 | Exposition Building, Portland, Maine, USA | W UD/10 |
| 1970-06-11 | Benny Huertas | 13–12–3 | Exposition Building, Portland, Maine, USA | L TKO/10 |
| 1970-05-21 | Doc McClendon | 2–2–1 | Exposition Building, Portland, Maine, USA | W UD/10 |
| 1970-04-30 | Ivelaw Eastman | 11–10–0 | Exposition Building, Portland, Maine, USA | W UD/10 |
| 1969-12-11 | Ken Campbell[b] | 11–2–0 | Exposition Building, Portland, Maine, USA | W KO/7 |
| 1969-11-20 | Mike Langlois | 0–1–1 | Exposition Building, Portland, Maine, USA | W KO/4 |
| 1969-11-06 | Ken Campbell[b] | 10–2–0 | Exposition Building, Portland, Maine, USA | L PTS/10 |
| 1969-06-26 | Sammy Goss | 6–0–0 | Exposition Building, Portland, Maine, USA | L SD/10 |
| 1969-04-10 | Leo DiFiore[c] | 35–5–1 | Exposition Building, Portland, Maine, USA | W UD/10 |
| 1968-12-12 | Mando Ramos | 23–3–0 | Olympic Auditorium, Los Angeles, California, USA | L TKO/2 |
| 1968-11-21 | Johnny Bean | 16–26-2 | Exposition Building, Portland, Maine, USA | L UD/10 |
| 1968-10-24 | Durango Kid | 11–5–1 | Exposition Building, Portland, Maine, USA | W UD/10 |
| 1968-08-15 | Jesus Alicia | 6–14–4 | Exposition Building, Portland, Maine, USA | W PTS/10 |
| 1968-07-25 | Mike Cruz | 14–20–5 | Exposition Building, Portland, Maine, USA | W UD/10 |
| 1968-06-20 | Sandy Seabrooke | 14–31–15 | Portland, Maine, USA | W TKO/7 |
| 1968-05-23 | Al Romano | 12–5–0 | Exposition Building, Portland, Maine, USA | W UD/10 |

| 1968-05-02 | Petey Dowd | 6–3–1 | Exposition Building, Portland, Maine, USA | W TKO/5 |
|---|---|---|---|---|
| 1968-03-23 | Gabe LaMarca | 14–4–3 | Arena, Boston, Massachusetts, USA | L SD/10 |
| 1968-02-14 | Billy McCluskey[c] | 9–0–0 | Exposition Building, Portland, Maine, USA | W UD/10 |
| 1967-12-18 | Gabe LaMarca | 13–4–3 | Boston Garden, Boston, Massachusetts, USA | L SD/10 |
| 1967-10-09 | Robert Hinton | 0–1–0 | Worcester, Massachusetts, USA | W SD/10 |
| 1967-05-25 | Hector Rodriguez | 16–30–1 | Exposition Building, Portland, Maine, USA | W SD/8 |
| 1967-04-14 | Bolo Martinez | 0–6–1 | Arena, Boston, Massachusetts, USA | W UD/10 |
| 1967-03-18 | Benny James | 3–6–0 | Arena, Boston, Massachusetts, USA | W UD/10 |
| 1967-02-06 | Jackie Burke | 13–5–0 | Boston Garden, Boston, Massachusetts, USA | W UD/10 |
| 1966-12-05 | Paddy Read | 26–24–0 | Mechanics Hall, Worcester, Massachusetts, USA | W UD/10 |
| 1966-11-14 | Paddy Read | 26–23–0 | Boston Garden, Boston, Massachusetts, USA | W UD/8 |
| 1966-10-24 | Ronnie Butts | 7–14–1 | Mechanics Hall, Worcester, Massachusetts, USA | W TKO/2 |
| 1966-10-17 | Dick Peterson | 1–3–0 | Mechanics Hall, Worcester, Massachusetts, USA | W TKO/2 |
| 1966-10-06 | Benny James | 1–6–0 | Exposition Building, Portland, Maine, USA | L SD/8 |
| 1966-10-03 | Arthur Butts | 1–3–2 | Mechanics Hall, Worcester, Massachusetts, USA | W TKO/3 |
| 1966-06-23 | Jackie Burke | 13–2–0 | Portland, Maine, USA | W UD/10 |
| 1966-06-09 | Paddy Read | 26–21–0 | Exposition Building, Portland, Maine, USA | W UD/10 |
| 1966-05-26 | Hector Rodriguez | 16–29–1 | Exposition Building, Portland, Maine, USA | W UD/10 |
| 1966-05-12 | Hector Rodriguez | 15–29–1 | Exposition Building, Portland, Maine, USA | L SD/10 |
| 1966-03-28 | Jackie Burke | 11–1–0 | City Hall, Lewiston, Maine, USA | L MD/10 |
| 1966-02-10 | Tommy Haden[d] | 13–13–0 | Exposition Building, Portland, Maine, USA | W UD/10 |

| 1966-01-27 | Tommy Haden | 13–12–0 | Exposition Building, Portland, Maine, USA | W UD/6 |
| 1965-11-22 | Chickie Garcia | 1–1–0 | Boston Garden, Boston, Massachusetts, USA | W KO/2 |
| 1965-11-01 | M. C. Cordova | 5–1–1 | Boston Garden, Boston, Massachusetts, USA | W UD/4 |
| 1965-10-25 | Jay McCombs | 9–0–0 | Mechanics Hall, Worcester, Massachusetts, USA | L PTS/4 |
| 1965-10-15 | Chickie Garcia | 1–0–0 | Arena, Boston, Massachusetts, USA | W UD/4 |
| 1965-09-11 | Joe Rivera |  | Arena, Boston, Massachusetts, USA | W UD/4 |

[a] USA New England welterweight title
[b] USA New England lightweight title
[c] USA New England super featherweight title
[d] USA New England featherweight title

## DICKY EKLUND (LOWELL, MASSACHUSETTS). CAREER RECORD: 19–10, 4 KNOCKOUTS.

| Date | Opponent | Opponent's Record (W–L–D) | Location | Result/ Round |
| --- | --- | --- | --- | --- |
| 1985-05-30 | James Lucas | 14–3–0 | Cumberland County Civic Center, Portland, Maine, USA | W UD/10 |
| 1983-10-25 | James Lucas[a] | 10–2–0 | Cumberland County Civic Center, Portland, Maine, USA | W SD/12 |
| 1983-09-22 | Reggie Miller | 12–0–0 | McNeese State College, Lake Charles, Louisiana, USA | L UD/10 |
| 1983-08-11 | Terry Crawley | 7–3–1 | Cape Cod Coliseum, South Yarmouth, Massachusetts, USA | W SD/10 |
| 1982-09-16 | Robert Sawyer | 10–5–0 | Sands Casino Hotel, Atlantic City, New Jersey, USA | L PTS/12 |
| 1982-07-31 | Jeff Passero | 16–4–1 | Bally's Park Place Hotel Casino, Atlantic City, New Jersey, USA | W PTS/8 |
| 1982-07-14 | Cesar Guzman | 0–4–0 | Dorchester, Massachusetts, USA | W PTS/8 |
| 1982-01-07 | Kevin Howard | 12–2–1 | Sands Casino Hotel, Atlantic City, New Jersey, USA | L SD/10 |

| | | | | |
|---|---|---|---|---|
| 1981-10-27 | Chris Clarke* | 21–2–0 | Halifax Metro Center, Halifax, Nova Scotia, Canada | L SD/10 |
| 1981-08-25 | Allen Clarke | 21–4–1 | Halifax Metro Center, Halifax, Nova Scotia, Canada | W KO/9 |
| 1981-02-10 | C. J. Faison | 12–13–0 | Paul Sauvé Arena, Montreal, Quebec, Canada | W KO/1 |
| 1980-06-20 | Fernando Fernandez | 16–3–1 | Boston Garden, Boston, Massachusetts, USA | L SD/10 |
| 1979-12-04 | Dave "Boy" Green | 32–2–0 | Empire Pool, Wembley, London, United Kingdom | L PTS/10 |
| 1979-08-18 | Fernando Fernandez | 14–2–1 | Lowell Auditorium, Lowell, Massachusetts, USA | W PTS/10 |
| 1978-07-18 | Sugar Ray Leonard | 12–0–0 | Hynes Auditorium, Boston, Massachusetts, USA | L UD/10 |
| 1978-03-04 | Willie Rodriguez | 12–2–0 | Boston Garden, Boston, Massachusetts, USA | L SD/8 |
| 1978-01-16 | Al Cruz | 0–1–0 | Waltham, Massachusetts, USA | W KO/5 |
| 1977-02-24 | Erkki Meronen | 30–1–0 | Idrottshuset, Copenhagen, Denmark | L PTS/6 |
| 1976-10-30 | Rufus Miller | 6–0–1 | East Hartford High School Gymnasium, East Hartford, Connecticut, USA | W UD/8 |
| 1976-09-20 | Mike Michaud | 6–1–0 | Golden Banana Club, Peabody, Massachusetts, USA | W SD/8 |
| 1976-06-24 | Randy Milton | 10–2–2 | Wallingford, Massachusetts, USA | W UD/6 |
| 1976-04-26 | Jose Carlos Garcia | 5–15–0 | Boston Garden, Boston, Massachusetts, USA | W UD/6 |
| 1976-02-21 | Charlie Benjamin | 1–3–1 | Waterbury, Connecticut, USA | W PTS/6 |
| 1976-01-31 | Terry Rondeau | 29–27–0 | State Armory, Waterbury, Connecticut, USA | W PTS/6 |
| 1975-12-20 | Jose Papo Melendez | 3–6–0 | Hynes Auditorium, Boston, Massachusetts, USA | W UD/4 |
| 1975-11-21 | Avelino Dos Reis | 4–2–0 | Providence, Rhode Island, USA | W KO/3 |
| 1975-11-06 | Eddie Hudson | 0–1–0 | Portland, Maine, USA | W UD/4 |
| 1975-09-30 | Doug Romano | 0–1–0 | Boston Garden, Boston, Massachusetts, USA | W UD/4 |

| 1975-08-26 | Joe DeFayette | 6–1–1 | Sargent Field, New Bedford, Massachusetts, USA | L SD/6 |
|---|---|---|---|---|

[a] USA New England welterweight title

## JOE GATTI (BAYONNE, NEW JERSEY). CAREER RECORD: 30–8, 22 KNOCK-OUTS.

| Date | Opponent | Opponent's Record (W–L–D) | Location | Result/ Round |
|---|---|---|---|---|
| 2002-08-24 | Sven Ottke[a] | 27–0–0 | Leipziger Arena, Leipzig, Sachsen, Germany | L TKO/9 |
| 2002-03-01 | Tim Shocks | 21–11–1 | Foxwoods Resort, Mashantucket, Connecticut, USA | W TKO/4 |
| 2001-07-10 | Alex Hilton | 37–6–0 | Molson Centre, Montreal, Quebec, Canada | W TKO/5 |
| 2001-03-02 | Roberto Dellapenna | 7–3–1 | Molson Centre, Montreal, Quebec, Canada | W UD/8 |
| 1999-01-02 | Allen Smith[b] | 17–9–3 | Zofingen-Aarau, Switzerland | W TKO/3 |
| 1998-10-01 | Kelvin Prather | 9–11–1 | Newark, New Jersey, USA | W TKO/2 |
| 1998-02-28 | Salvatore Di Salvatore[c] | 16–4–1 | Zofingen-Aarau, Switzerland | L TKO/7 |
| 1996-09-26 | Oswaldo Bello | 6–4–2 | Medieval Times, Lyndhurst, New Jersey, USA | L TKO/3 |
| 1995-12-01 | Tim Dendy | 15–14–1 | Staten Island, New York, USA | W UD/10 |
| 1995-10-03 | Tim Bonds | 3–25–0 | Memphis, Tennessee, USA | W KO/1 |
| 1995-09-27 | Willie Kemp | 14–19–0 | Roxy, Boston, Massachusetts, USA | W PTS/6 |
| 1995-05-07 | James McGirt | 65–4–1 | Grand Theatre, Biloxi, Mississippi, USA | L TKO/5 |
| 1994-10-08 | James Stokes | 14–9–0 | Vernon, New Jersey, USA | W KO 1 |
| 1994-03-31 | Rafael Williams | 31–13–0 | Huntington Hilton Hotel, Melville, New York, USA | L UD/10 |
| 1994-02-05 | Mike Williams | 7–8–0 | Long Branch, New Jersey, USA | W TKO/2 |

| Date | Opponent | Record | Venue | Result |
|---|---|---|---|---|
| 1993-09-10 | Terry Norris[d] | 35–3–0 | Alamodome, San Antonio, Texas, USA | L TKO/1 |
| 1993-04-07 | Nate Woods | 6–2–0 | Newark, New Jersey, USA | W PTS/10 |
| 1993-03-06 | Oscar Noriega | 1–5–0 | Madison Square Garden, New York, New York, USA | W TKO/2 |
| 1992-11-14 | Terry Whittaker | 22–9–2 | McAfee, New Jersey, USA | W UD/10 |
| 1992-07-30 | Mike Williams | 7–5–0 | Waterloo Village, Stanhope, New Jersey, USA | W TKO/1 |
| 1991-12-05 | Glenn Odem | 7–3–0 | Quality Inn Hotel, Newark, New Jersey, USA | W TKO/1 |
| 1991-08-02 | Ken Hulsey | 11–5–1 | Quality Inn Hotel, Newark, New Jersey, USA | W KO/1 |
| 1991-06-10 | Ralph Moncrief | 25–14–0 | Meadowlands Convention Center, Secaucus, New Jersey, USA | W MD/10 |
| 1991-04-30 | Muhammad Shabazz | 15–11–0 | Blue Horizon, Philadelphia, Pennsylvania, USA | W TKO/1 |
| 1991-03-25 | Matt Farrago | 25–1–1 | Meadowlands Convention Center, Secaucus, New Jersey, USA | W KO/2 |
| 1991-01-08 | Aaron Smith | 5–4–1 | Blue Horizon, Philadelphia, Pennsylvania, USA | W TKO/3 |
| 1990-10-22 | Brinatty Maquilon | 11–7–0 | Trump Plaza Hotel, Atlantic City, New Jersey, USA | W UD/8 |
| 1990-08-17 | Eric Holland | 6–8–2 | Quality Inn Hotel, Newark, New Jersey, USA | W TKO/2 |
| 1990-07-08 | Michael Ward | 5–1–0 | Harrah's Marina Hotel Casino, Atlantic City, New Jersey, USA | L UD/6 |
| 1990-05-08 | Lynn Robertson | 0–1–0 | Harrah's Marina Hotel Casino, Atlantic City, New Jersey, USA | W KO/2 |
| 1990-04-07 | Dwayne Lattimore | 0–3–0 | Beckley, West Virginia, USA | W KO/1 |
| 1990-03-16 | Ferris Christian | 2–1–0 | Essex County College, Newark, New Jersey, USA | W TKO/1 |
| 1989-06-27 | Jacques DeBlois | 5–12–2 | Paul Sauvé Arena, Montreal, Quebec, Canada | W KO/2 |
| 1988-11-04 | Donnie Giron | 1–1–0 | Las Vegas Hilton, Hilton Center, Las Vegas, Nevada, USA | L TKO/1 |
| 1988-07-29 | Calvin Christensen | 2–0–0 | Caesars Palace, Sports Pavilion, Las Vegas, Nevada, USA | W TKO/2 |

| 1988-06-25 | Lemark Davis | 3–0–0 | Trump Plaza Hotel, Atlantic City, New Jersey, USA | W UD/4 |
|---|---|---|---|---|
| 1987-06-27 | Joe Doby | | Forum, Montreal, Quebec, Canada | W TKO/2 |
| 1987-04-29 | James McNee | 3–1–0 | Paul Sauvé Arena, Montreal, Quebec, Canada | W TKO/2 |

[a] IBF World super middleweight title
[b] IBC Intercontinental light heavyweight title
[c] IBC light heavyweight title
[d] WBC World super welterweight title

*Tables reprinted with permission from Boxrec.com.*

# NOTES

## 1. "I ALWAYS WONDERED WHAT IT WOULD BE LIKE TO FIGHT MY TWIN"

1. Bob Halloran, *Irish Thunder: The Hard Life and Times of Micky Ward* (Guilford, CT: Globe Pequot, 2007).

2. Micky Ward and Joe Layden, *A Warrior's Heart: The True Story of Life before and beyond* The Fighter (New York: Berkley, 2012).

3. Joyce Carol Oates, "The Fighter's Cruel Art," *New York Review*, 3 February 2011.

## 2. MICKY

1. Christine Lewis, "Boxing: Larry Carney," *Merrimack Valley Magazine*, November/December 2010.

2. Lyle Moran, "Former Lowell Boxer Wraps Up DPW Career as Champ," *Lowell Sun*, 9 March 2012.

3. Moran, "Former Lowell Boxer Wraps Up DPW Career as Champ."

4. Bob Halloran, *Irish Thunder: The Hard Life and Times of Micky Ward* (Guilford, CT: Globe Pequot, 2007).

5. Dicky spelled his first name "Dickie" throughout most of his life and boxing career. He changed the spelling to "Dicky"—to match the spelling of his brother, Micky—while doing publicity for the Hollywood movie *The Fighter*, a biopic of the brothers' lives. He continues to use "Dicky" as his preferred spelling, which is why we settled on that option for this book.

## 3. ARTURO

1. *Arturo Gatti: The People's Champion*, 2009, Concrete Cinema.
2. Evan Rothman, "A Puncher's Chance: Arturo Gatti, New Jersey's Favorite Fighter, Keeps Firing," *New Jersey Monthly*, 4 February 2008.
3. *Arturo Gatti: The People's Champion*, 1993, HBO Sports, Pardeep Dhillon.
4. *Arturo Gatti: The People's Champion*.
5. *Arturo Gatti: The People's Champion*.
6. *Legendary Nights: The Tale of Arturo Gatti vs. Micky Ward*, 2013, HBO Sports.
7. *Legendary Nights*.
8. "Ray Mancini: Pride of Youngstown," *Ringside Boxing Show*, 8 November 2015, http://ringsideboxingshow.podbean.com/e/ray-mancini-pride-of-youngstown/.
9. Franz Lidz, "Hooks and Splatters," *Sports Illustrated*, 26 July 2004.

## 4. BROTHER'S KEEPER

1. Micky Ward and Joe Layden, *A Warrior's Heart: The True Story of Life before and beyond* The Fighter (New York: Berkley, 2012).
2. Bob Halloran, *Irish Thunder: The Hard Life and Times of Micky Ward* (Guilford, CT: Globe Pequot, 2007).

## 5. ROLLER COASTER

1. *Arturo Gatti: The People's Champion*, 1993, HBO Sports, Pardeep Dhillon.
2. "In Depth: Gabriel Ruelas," *Ringside Boxing Show*, 2013, http://ringsideboxingshow.podbean.com/e/in-depth-gabriel-ruelas.
3. "In Depth: Angel Manfredy," *Ringside Boxing Show*, 5 January 2014, http://ringsideboxingshow.podbean.com/e/in-depth-angel-manfredy.
4. "Catching 'Mighty' Ivan Robinson," *Real Combat Media*, 5 May 2012, http://realcombatmedia.com/2012/03/catching-mighty-ivan-robinson. Subsequent quotes from Robinson were also taken from this source.
5. Ray Leonard and Michael Arkus, *The Big Fight: My Life In and Out of the Ring* (New York: Berkley, 2011).

## 6. BLOOD IS NOT ALWAYS THICKER

1. Micky Ward and Joe Layden, *A Warrior's Heart: The True Story of Life before and beyond* The Fighter (New York: Berkley, 2012).

2. Ward and Layden, *A Warrior's Heart.*

3. Bob Halloran, *Irish Thunder: The Hard Life and Times of Micky Ward* (Guilford, CT: Globe Pequot, 2007).

4. Halloran, *Irish Thunder.*

5. Ward and Layden, *A Warrior's Heart.*

6. Halloran, *Irish Thunder.*

7. "Dicky Eklund, Micky Ward's Brother," *Ringside Boxing Show*, 13 November 2011, http://ringsideboxingshow.podbean.com/e/dicky-eklund-micky-wards-brother/.

8. *High on Crack Street: The Lost Lives of Lowell*, 1995, HBO, DCTV.

9. Ward and Layden, *A Warrior's Heart.*

10. Halloran, *Irish Thunder.*

11. "Dicky Eklund, Micky Ward's Brother."

12. "Dicky Eklund, Micky Ward's Brother."

13. Halloran, *Irish Thunder.*

14. Ward and Layden, *A Warrior's Heart.*

## 7. CROSSROADS

1. Micky Ward and Joe Layden, *A Warrior's Heart: The True Story of Life before and beyond* The Fighter (New York: Berkley, 2012).

2. "Dicky Eklund, Micky Ward's Brother," *Ringside Boxing Show*, 13 November 2011, http://ringsideboxingshow.podbean.com/e/dicky-eklund-micky-wards-brother/.

3. Ward and Layden, *A Warrior's Heart.*

4. "'Irish' Micky Ward v. Jesse James Leija, 5/1/02," *YouTube*, 3 July 2015, https://www.youtube.com/watch?v=iGdh0sqhwuM.

5. Ward and Layden, *A Warrior's Heart.*

## 8. REBIRTH

1. Ryan Songalia, "Arturo Gatti Friend Mike Sciara Tells Arturo Gatti Stories," *YouTube*, 7 September 2011, https://www.youtube.com/watch?v=fj0YaL4bY50.

2. *Legendary Nights: The Tale of Arturo Gatti vs. Micky Ward*, 2013, HBO Sports.

3. Mitch Abramson, "Overmatched Joey Gamache Blames State for Brutal Bout with Gatti That Left Him Damaged, Depressed," *New York Daily News*, 21 July 2009.

4. Mitch Abramson, "Damaged Gamache Feels Weight of the World," *New York Daily News*, 21 July 2009.

## 9. "IT'S GOING TO BE A GREAT FIGHT"

1. "Boxing Legendary Nights: Arturo Gatti v Micky Ward Trilogy" (documentary), *YouTube*, 14 December 2014, https://www.youtube.com/watch?v=TYtCZDqepzE.

2. "Boxing Legendary Nights."

## 10. BEAUTIFUL, UGLY, AND DANGEROUS

1. Unless otherwise noted, quotes were taken from the HBO telecast via the HBO microphone.

## 11. "LET'S DO IT AGAIN"

1. "Boxing Legendary Nights: Arturo Gatti v Micky Ward Trilogy" (documentary), *YouTube*, 14 December 2014, https://www.youtube.com/watch?v=TYtCZDqepzE.

2. "Boxing Legendary Nights."

3. "Boxing Legendary Nights."

4. *Legendary Nights: The Tale of Arturo Gatti vs. Micky Ward*, 2013, HBO Sports.

5. Unless otherwise noted, quotes were taken from the HBO telecast via the HBO microphone.

6. Micky Ward and Joe Layden, *A Warrior's Heart: The True Story of Life before and beyond* The Fighter (New York: Berkley, 2012).

## 12. BLOOD AND GUTS

1. "Boxing Legendary Nights: Arturo Gatti v Micky Ward Trilogy" (documentary), *YouTube*, 14 December 2014, https://www.youtube.com/watch?v=TYtCZDqepzE.

2. Dennis Taylor, "In Depth: Buddy McGirt," *Ringside Boxing Show*, 7 June 2015, http://ringsideboxingshow.podbean.com/e/in-depth-buddy-mcgirt/ .

3. "Boxing Legendary Nights."

4. Unless otherwise noted, quotes were taken from the HBO telecast via the HBO microphone.

5. *Legendary Nights: The Tale of Arturo Gatti vs. Micky Ward*, 2013, HBO Sports.

## 13. FRIENDS

1. *Legendary Nights: The Tale of Arturo Gatti vs. Micky Ward*, 2013, HBO Sports.

2. Micky Ward and Joe Layden, *A Warrior's Heart: The True Story of Life before and beyond* The Fighter (New York: Berkley, 2012).

3. Eric Raskin, "The World Will Never Stop Paying Tribute to Arturo Gatti and Micky Ward, Nor Should It," *Grantland.com*, 18 October 2013, http://grantland.com/the-triangle/the-world-will-never-stop-paying-tribute-to-arturo-gatti-and-micky-ward-nor-should-it/.

4. Ward and Layden, *A Warrior's Heart*.

## 14. REUNION

1. "Dicky Eklund, Micky Ward's Brother," *Ringside Boxing Show*, 13 November 2011, http://ringsideboxingshow.podbean.com/e/dicky-eklund-micky-wards-brother/ .

2. *Legendary Nights: The Tale of Arturo Gatti vs. Micky Ward*, 2013, HBO Sports.

## 15. AN ENDURING MYSTERY

1. "Arturo Gatti's Last Fight," 25 September 2011, *48 Hours Mystery*, CBS.

2. "Arturo Gatti's Last Fight."

3. "Arturo Gatti's Last Fight."

4. "Arturo Gatti's Last Fight."

5. "Inside the Gatti v. Gatti Case," 3 August 2014, *Fifth Estate*, CBC News.

6. "Catching 'Mighty' Ivan Robinson," *Real Combat Media*, 5 March 2012, http://realcombatmedia.com/2012/03/catching-mighty-ivan-robinson.

7. "Inside the Gatti v. Gatti Case."

8. "The Trials of Arturo Gatti's Widow," 26 March 2012, *48 Hours Mystery*, CBS.

9. Keith Idec, "Inside Look: Arturo Gatti's Death Has Torn His Family Apart," *Boxing Scene*, 2 October 2010, http://www.boxingscene.com/inside-look-arturo-gattis-death-torn-his-family-apart--31453.

10. Matthew Turbide, "Arturo Gatti n'aurait pas ete tue," *Journal de Montreal*, 9 November 2011.

11. Les Perreaux, "Arturo Gatti Suicide Skeptics Evade Boxer's Dark Truths," *Toronto Globe and Mail*, 26 September 2011.

12. Perreaux, "Arturo Gatti Suicide Skeptics Evade Boxer's Dark Truths."

13. Domenic Fazioli, "New Evidence Re-opens Investigation into Death of Gatti," *Global News*, 25 February 2013.

## EPILOGUE

1. "Dicky Eklund, Micky Ward's Brother," *Ringside Boxing Show*, 13 November 2011, http://ringsideboxingshow.podbean.com/e/dicky-eklund-micky-wards-brother/ .

2. "Dicky Eklund, Micky Ward's Brother."

## APPENDIX A

1. Carlo Rotella, "Arturo Gatti: On the Ropes," *New York Times Magazine*, 23 December 2009.

2. Clifton Brown, "If Gatti's Fighting, Figure on Brutal Bout," *New York Times*, 22 July 2006.

3. Richard Goldstein, "Arturo Gatti, Fearless Boxer Known for Relentless Violence, Dies at 37," *New York Times*, 12 July 2009.

4. Brown, "If Gatti's Fighting, Figure on Brutal Bout."

5. Steve Springer, "Gatti Ready to Take a Shot," *Los Angeles Times*, 24 March 2001.

6. Jay Searcy, "Robinson Takes Bout with Class," *Philadelphia Inquirer*, 14 December 1998.

7. Jay Searcy, "This Champ's Toughest Foe Is the Scale," *Philadelphia Inquirer*, 16 January 1998.

8. Don Steinberg, "Gatti May Retire after Brutal Loss," *Philadelphia Inquirer*, 24 July 2006.

9. Bernard Fernandez, "Arturo Gatti's Greatness Is in the Eye of the Beholder," *Sweet Science*, 5 June 2013.

10. Bernard Fernandez, "Leading with His Face Has Worked for Gatti So Far," *Philadelphia Daily News*, 15 January 1998.

11. Michael Woods, "The End of the Road for Gatti," *Sweet Science*, 13 July 2007.

12. Eric Raskin, "The World Will Never Stop Paying Tribute to Arturo Gatti," *Grantland.com*, 18 October 2013, http://grantland.com/the-triangle/the-world-will-never-stop-paying-tribute-to-arturo-gatti-and-micky-ward-nor-should-it/ .

13. Luke O'Brien, "What the Furious Ninth Round of Gatti–Ward 1 Tells Us about Life," *Deadspin.com*, 23 March 2011, http://deadspin.com/5784930/what-the-furious-ninth-round-of-gatti-ward-1-says-about-life .

14. John Rawling, "Arturo Gatti: World Champion Boxer Whose Blood-and-Guts Style Was Loved by Fans," *Guardian*, 13 July 2009.

15. Cheekay Brandon, "The Measure of Men," *Boxing.com*, 17 May 2012, http://www.boxing.com/may_18_2002_the_measure_of_men.html .

16. Jim Lampley, *HBO World Championship Boxing* live telecast of Gatti–Ward fight, 18 May 2002.

17. Kathy Duva, HBO's *Legendary Nights*, 17 October 2013.

18. Ron Borges, "'Legendary' Status for Micky Ward, Arturo Gatti," *Boston Herald*, 17 October 2013.

19. Jerry Izenberg, "Jersey Guy Arturo Gatti Packed a Special Punch," *New Jersey Star-Ledger*, 13 July 2009.

20. Izenberg, "Jersey Guy Arturo Gatti Packed a Special Punch."

21. Izenberg, "Jersey Guy Arturo Gatti Packed a Special Punch."

22. Jeff Powell, "Mayweather Could Learn a Thing or Two from Ward and Gatti," *Daily Mail*, 31 January 2011.

23. John Scully, "More Fighters Comment on Arturo Gatti," *ConvictedArtist.com*, July 2009, http://www.convictedartistmagazine.com/boxing-news/187-more-fighters-comment-on-arturo-gatti.html .

24. Micky Ward, "Micky Ward Believes Arturo Gatti Is Hall of Fame Material," *ThaBoxingVoice.com*, 9 October 2012, http://thaboxingvoice.com/micky-ward-believes-arturo-gatti-is-hall-of-fame-material/5010?var=no .

25. Tim Starks, "Arturo Gatti, 'The Human Highlight Film,' Found Dead in Brazil," *Queensberry Rules*, 11 July 2009.

26. Ivan Robinson, "When I Boxed a Legend: Ivan Robinson Recalls Boxing Arturo Gatti," *Examiner.com*, 6 June 2013, http://www.examiner.com/article/when-i-boxed-a-legend-ivan-robinson-recalls-boxing-arturo-gatti .

27. Dan Rafael, "Honoree Arturo Gatti: 1972–2009," *New Jersey Boxing Hall of Fame*, 12 November 2009, http://www.njboxinghof.org/arturo-gatti/ .

28. Andy McCullough, "Former New Jersey Boxing Champ Arturo Gatti Found Dead in Brazilian Resort," *New Jersey Star-Ledger*, 12 July 2009.

29. Nathaniel Vinton, "Life of Fearless Working-Class 'Fighter' Micky Ward Becomes Stuff of Hollywood Dreams," *New York Daily News*, 26 December 2010.

30. Vinton, "Life of Fearless Working-Class 'Fighter' Micky Ward."

31. Ed Godfrey, "Collected Wisdom: Micky Ward, Retired Boxer," *News-OK.com*, 4 February 2012, http://newsok.com/article/3646394 .

32. Thomas Hauser, "Irish Micky Ward: The Fighter Speaks Out," *Irish America*, February/March 2011.

33. Thomas, "Irish Micky Ward."

34. Thomas, "Irish Micky Ward."

35. Adam Berlin, "The Hard Life and Times of Micky Ward . . . Mladinich," *Sweet Science*, 13 December 2007.

36. Michael Woods, "Here's What Micky Ward Would Like You to Take from 'Gatti–Ward' on HBO," *Sweet Science*, 17 October 2013.

37. Mark Connor, "Irish Thunder Biographer Discusses Micky Ward's Fall, Rise," *Wild Geese*, 19 January 2013.

38. Louis C.K., "Louis C.K. Explains His Friendship with Micky Ward," *www.checkhookboxing.com*, 14 January 2014, http://checkhookboxing.com/index.php?threads/louis-c-k-explains-his-friendship-with-micky-ward-his-love-of-boxing.32704/ .

39. Jim Lampley, *HBO World Championship Boxing* live telecast of Gatti–Ward fight, 7 June 2003.

40. Larry Merchant, *HBO World Championship Boxing* live telecast of Gatti–Ward fight, 7 June 2003.

41. Larry Merchant, *HBO World Championship Boxing* live telecast of Gatti–Ward fight, 18 May 2002.

# INDEX

# ABOUT THE AUTHORS

**Dennis Taylor** has been a professional journalist for more than 40 years with six newspapers, in Colorado, North Carolina, and California, as well as *Denver Magazine*, *Pebble Beach Magazine*, *Carmel Magazine*, and multiple other publications. Taylor is editor/publisher of www. ringsideboxingshow.comand host of *The Ringside Boxing Show*, a world-wide Internet radio program that airs Sundays at 4 p.m. Pacific at www. radiomonterey.com. He has written for www.boxing.comandwww.ringtv. com. Taylor also is author of *A Puncher's Chance*, a nonfiction boxing book, and *The Miracle Myth*, a humor novel, both available at www. dennistaylorbooks.com. He lives near Monterey, California.

**John J. Raspanti** is chief lead writer for both www.maxboxing. comandwww.doghouseboxing.com, and has been a contributor to www. ringtv.com. *Intimate Warfare: The True Story of the Arturo Gatti and Micky Ward Boxing Trilogy* is his first published work. Raspanti is a Southern California native and a resident of the San Francisco Bay Area.

## ABOUT THE PHOTOGRAPHER

It is, perhaps, fortuitous that **Ed Mulholland**'s beloved alma mater, Rutgers University, dresses its athletes in scarlet. The bright red cap he proudly wears as he shoots boxing from the ring apron of HBO-televised events is splattered with the blood (not to mention sweat and spittle) of many of the greatest fighters of a generation: Mike Tyson, Wladimir

Klitschko, Roy Jones Jr., Felix Trinidad, Bernard Hopkins, Joe Calzaghe, Evander Holyfield. To find more Hall of Fame DNA, you probably need to go to Canastota.

Mulholland, who shot the photos displayed in this book (including the cover image), said he must be the "luckiest photographer on earth"—perhaps the only professional sports shooter in the United States who didn't cut his or her teeth in the blowing snow during Friday night high school football games.

Mulholland was strictly a hobby photographer when his brother Scott got a pair of free ringside tickets one night to a small boxing event in Bushkill, Pennsylvania.

"I brought a camera with me, took some photos, and, kind of as a goof, I sent them off to FightNews, only because that was a website I looked at all the time," he recalled. "Next thing I know, they're calling me up, saying, 'We'd like to have you shoot some fights for us, if you're interested.'"

Two weeks later, he was in Reading, Pennsylvania, representing FightNews, when Ricardo Mayorga starched Andrew "Six Heads" Lewis in the fifth round of a WBA welterweight title bout that was televised by Showtime.

"Afterward, at the press conference, Mayorga came to the podium with the WBA belt around his waist, a Budweiser in one hand, and a cigarette in the other, and I thought, 'Wow, there's a unique photo,'" Mulholland remembered. "I got the shot, and it wound up being my first *Sports Illustrated* photo. And, that's how I got my start."

And it was only a start. Three months later, he was cleaning blood off his lenses from one of the most spectacular fights in boxing history, Gatti–Ward I, at Mohegan Sun Casino in Uncasville, Connecticut. Gatti and Ward, of course, would do it twice more (with Mulholland on the ring apron in his red Rutgers hat), creating a trilogy that sits atop every credible historian's list.

After two years of shooting for FightNews, Mulholland got another out-of-the-blue call from a representative of Electronic Arts (EA Sports), the video game company famous for its *Fight Night* series.

"Those guys had brought Gatti and Ward together in Chicago for a studio shoot to create a cover photo for *Fight Night 3*," Mulholland said. "Apparently, Arturo and Micky had gone out on the town the night before and partied pretty hard, and neither of them looked very good for the photos the next day. The company decided they were unusable."

Instead, the company paid Mulholland for a classic action shot of the two gladiators, forehead to forehead, and turned the photo into the box cover. (That same image graces the cover of this book.)

"The atmosphere before a major fight is absolutely tremendous. I don't know if another sport can match that," said Mulholland, who has shot from rink-side at the Stanley Cup Finals and from a front-row post at the Super Bowl.

"I love fight week in Las Vegas, at a place like the MGM Grand, because there's such a buzz, and because it all happens in the same building. You see great fighters and famous fight people walking around everywhere. They're riding the elevators with you. And the fans are so excited. There's such a buzz," he added.

"Whenever Ricky Hatton fought in Vegas, you'd go to bed on a Thursday night, when there were a few fighters and journalists wandering around the hotel, then you'd go down to breakfast at 8 o'clock Friday morning and find all of these British guys, just off the plane, drinking, and carousing, and singing songs. You'd think you were in the middle of Manchester."

Mulholland's job as HBO's boxing photographer has taken him to unique international venues. These include the second-largest bullring in the world in Mexico City for a Canelo Alvarez fight; Mannheim, Germany, for a Wladimir Klitschko defense; England's Wembley Stadium for Carl Froch versus George Groves (where Groves arrived in a double-decker bus); and Montreal, where fans ate dinner at high-priced ringside tables while they watched the carnage.

"But I'll tell you, for my money, Miguel Cotto at Madison Square Garden, during the week of the Puerto Rican Day Parade, tops everything," said Mulholland, who won the Boxing Writers Association's Photo of the Year Award for Best Feature Photo (2005) and Best Action Photo (2007). "That atmosphere is just another world."

A close contender, he commented, would be any Arturo Gatti fight at Atlantic City's Boardwalk Hall.

Mulholland shot the final 10 fights of Gatti's sensational, Hall of Fame career, beginning with the first in the epic trilogy against Ward. He befriended Gatti and members of his inner circle along the way, imbibed with the champ at the Toga Bar at Caesars Palace, and came away with a treasured souvenir that could only be fully appreciated by a true-blue boxing fan in a blood-splattered Rutgers hat.

"I have the bloody hand wraps from Arturo's last fight. They were given to me at the postfight press conference by one of his trainers," Mulholland related. "I've shadowboxed and framed them, and they're hanging from my basement wall. They are absolutely the prize of my collection."